KU-676-088

How the *Just so Stories* Were Made

BAINTE DEN STOC

WITHDRAWN FROM
DÚN LAOGHAIRE-RATHDOWN COUNTY
LIBRARY STOCK

By the same author

Mervyn Peake: A Biographical and Critical Exploration (1974)

The Edwardian Novelists (1982)

H.G. Wells (1985)

Joseph Conrad's *Lord Jim*: A Study (1988)

Virginia Woolf: The Major Novels (1992)

The Life of Joseph Conrad: A Critical Biography (1995)

John Ruskin: No Wealth but Life – A Biography (2000)

Lady Trevelyan and the Pre-Raphaelite Brotherhood (2006)

Tennyson: To Strive, to Seek, to Find – A Biography (2012)

As editor

Joseph Conrad, *Lord Jim* (Oxford World's Classics, 1983)

Joseph Conrad, *Victory* (Oxford World's Classics, 1986)

The Art of Literary Biography (1996)

Shakespearean Continuities: Essays in Honour of E.A.J. Honigmann
(jointly with Tom Cain and Claire Lamont, 1997)

Victorian Literature (Yearbook of English Studies, 36.2, 2006)

From Decadent to Modernist: And Other Essays
(Yearbook of English Studies, 37.1, 2007)

How the *Just so Stories* Were Made

The Brilliance and Tragedy Behind Kipling's Celebrated Tales for Little Children

John Batchelor

YALE UNIVERSITY PRESS
NEW HAVEN AND LONDON

Copyright © 2021 John Batchelor

All rights reserved. This book may not be reproduced in whole or in part, in any form (beyond that copying permitted by Sections 107 and 108 of the U.S. Copyright Law and except by reviewers for the public press) without written permission from the publishers.

For information about this and other Yale University Press publications, please contact:
U.S. Office: sales.press@yale.edu yalebooks.com
Europe Office: sales@yaleup.co.uk yalebooks.co.uk

Set in Minion Pro by IDSUK (DataConnection) Ltd
Printed in Great Britain by TJ Books, Padstow, Cornwall

Library of Congress Control Number: 2020949868

ISBN 978-0-300-23718-4

A catalogue record for this book is available from the British Library.

10 9 8 7 6 5 4 3 2 1

MIX
Paper from
responsible sources
FSC® C013056
www.fsc.org

For Henrietta and for our grandchildren, Elise Batchelor, Adele Batchelor, Tara Benton, Luke Benton and Henry Batchelor

CONTENTS

ILLUSTRATIONS

Unless otherwise stated, images are from Rudyard Kipling, *The Just so Stories* (London: Macmillan, 1902).

Illustrations

Illustrations

PREFACE AND
ACKNOWLEDGEMENTS

Rudyard Kipling was a man of astonishing talent and energy, protean, wayward, brilliant, elusive and unpredictable. After a magical infancy in India he was plunged into a hell on earth at the mercy of a sadistic guardian in England, and then rescued by parental connections and his own prodigious talent to embark on a career as a writer and journalist in India at the age of 16. The volume known as the *Just so Stories* is in one sense the most perfect of his works of art. It was entirely under his own control, all the stories and images were created by him, and all the parts of his text support and complement each other. There is no other children's book quite like it.

I am very grateful to the Warden and Fellows of New College, Oxford, for their hospitality, encouragement and support during the period that I have worked on this book, and also in particular I would to thank the College's librarian, Christopher Skelton-Foord, for his constant and reliable help. I would also like to thank the British Library for access to the manuscript of the *Just so Stories*, the archivist and staff in charge of the Kipling archive held by the University of Sussex, and the officers of the National Trust for permission to reproduce images held in that collection. I would like to extend similar acknowledgement and thanks to the Victoria and Albert Museum and to the Landmark Trust, Vermont.

I am very grateful to Leonee Ormond, Harry Ricketts and Tom Shippey for the expertise and professionalism with which they have considered this project and read and commented on my text, and to the

Preface and Acknowledgements

editorial team at Yale headed by Julian Loose. Felicity Bryan, my literary agent who had represented all my books since 1988 and was wholly committed to this project, died a few months before it went to press. She is sadly missed by all who knew her.

My greatest debt is to my wife, Henrietta, who has encouraged and supported me through the writing of this and all my previous books.

Kidlington, Oxford, October 2020

1
HOW THE WHALE GOT HIS THROAT

In the sea, once upon a time, O my Best Beloved, there was a Whale, and he ate fishes. He ate the starfish and the garfish, and the crab and the dab, and the plaice and the dace, and the skate and his mate, and the mackereel and the pickereel, and the really truly twirly-whirly eel. All the fishes he could find in all the sea he ate with his mouth – so! Till at last there was only one small fish left in all the sea, and he was a small 'Stute Fish, and he swam a little behind the Whale's right ear, so as to be out of harm's way.

The Whale then 'stood up on his tail' and said 'I'm hungry', and the 'Stute Fish responded to this cue with a seemingly innocuous question: '"Noble and generous Cetacean, have you ever tasted Man?" "No," said the Whale, "What is it like?" "Nice," said the small 'Stute Fish. "Nice but nubbly."' Following directions from the 'Stute Fish the Whale 'swam and swam to latitude Fifty North, longitude Forty West, as fast as he could swim, and *on* a raft, *in* the middle of the sea, *with* nothing to wear except a pair of blue canvas breeches, a pair of suspenders [braces] (you must particularly remember the suspenders, Best Beloved), *and* a jack-knife, he found one single, solitary ship-wrecked Mariner, trailing his toes in the water.'[1] The story-teller here, addressing himself to his 'Best Beloved', echoes the narrator of E. W. Lane's *Arabian Nights' Entertainment* (1883), of which the Kiplings had a copy. The speaker is on intimate terms with his audience, and announces himself to the 'Best Beloved' as a genial father figure.

How the *Just so Stories* Were Made

The Whale swallows the Mariner and his raft 'and the suspenders (which you *must* not forget), *and* the jack-knife – He swallowed them all down into his warm, dark, inside cupboards, and then he smacked his lips – so, and turned round three times on his tail.' But the Mariner is a man of 'infinite-resource-and-sagacity': 'he jumped and he thumped and he bumped, and he pranced and he danced, and he banged and he clanged, and he hit and he bit, and he leaped and he creeped, and he prowled and he howled, and he hopped and he dropped, and he cried and he sighed, and he crawled and he bawled, and he stepped and he lepped, and he danced hornpipes where he shouldn't, and the Whale felt most unhappy indeed'.[2] The Whale calls 'down his own throat' to the Mariner: ' "Come out and behave yourself. I've got the hiccoughs." "Nay, nay!" said the Mariner. "Not so, but far otherwise. Take me to my natal-shore and the white-cliffs-of-Albion, and I'll think about it." And he began to dance more than ever.'[3]

So the Whale swims to 'the white-cliffs-of-Albion' and disgorges the Mariner. While inside the Whale's stomach (the Whale's 'warm, dark, inside cupboards') the Mariner has cut up his raft and made it into a wooden grill, or grating, to block the Whale's throat. The grating is held together by his 'suspenders': '*now* you know why you were not to forget the suspenders!' – with this announcement Kipling the conjuror reveals his methods; the rabbit comes out of the hat, so to speak. To crown his achievement the Mariner recites a '*sloka*' (the word refers to a verse form of the Sanskrit epics, here boiled down to two lines in an Irish accent):

> By means of a grating
> I have stopped your ating.

There is a fine image of the Whale swallowing the raft. The caption to this image begins: 'This is the picture of the Whale swallowing the Mariner with his infinite-resource-and-sagacity, and the raft and the jack-knife *and* his suspenders, which you must *not* forget.'[4] The raft in the manuscript presented problems of geometry and perspective which Kipling skilfully overcame. The manuscript tells us that the raft has 'tilted up' and Kipling

refined this in the printed text to 'tilted up *sideways*' (emphasis added), hence the sharp diagonal of the raft and the uncomfortable positions of the Mariner's right hand and right foot.

In the main narrative the Mariner is not named, but in the caption to this picture he and the Whale are both given names: 'The Whale's name was Smiler, and the Mariner was called Mr Henry Albert Bivvens, A.B.' The British Library's unpublished manuscript of the story has a variant of this: 'The Whale's name was Smiler, and the Mariner was called Mr O'Shea.'[5] (If Kipling had retained 'O'Shea' in the published text it would have laboured the point that the Mariner is Irish.) The next folio of the manuscript changes 'O'Shea' to 'Henry Alfred Bivvens' ('Albert' in the published text is a further variant).*

---

* Both 'Albert' and 'Alfred' were names which carried considerable resonance for late Victorians. Prince Albert was Queen Victoria's beloved consort who died young in 1861; 'Alfred' was the name of the Queen's great Laureate, Tennyson, whose *In Memoriam* became the Queen's favourite poem.

Like many a rural Irishman the Mariner has a strong mother. He 'went home to his Mother, who had given him leave to trail his toes in the water; and he married and lived happily ever afterward. So did the Whale. But from that day on, the grating in his throat, which he could neither cough up nor swallow down, prevented him eating anything except very, very small fish; and that is the reason why whales nowadays never eat men or boys or little girls.' Everything is itemised: the sailor takes his jack-knife home and is still wearing his blue canvas breeches, while the 'suspenders' which tie the grating are left inside the Whale's throat. 'And that is end of *that* tale.'[6]

How the Whale got his Throat

The 'end' of the tale is not in fact the end. There is an additional and final ending in the caption to the second picture. In this image the Whale is hunting for the 'Stute fish which is 'hiding among the roots of the big seaweed that grows in front of the Doors of the Equator'. We learn that 'the little 'Stute Fish's name was Pingle', and that the Whale 'never found the little 'Stute Fish till he got over his temper, and then they became good friends again'.[7]

The Whale's eye was drawn from life, observed by Kipling when he was crossing the Atlantic between England and Vermont. He and his wife lived in Vermont from 1892 to 1896, and during that period they made several crossings of the Atlantic: 'And we learned to loathe the cold North Atlantic more and more. On one trip our steamer came almost atop of a whale, who submerged just in time to clear us, and looked up into my face with an unforgettable little eye the size of a bullock's. [...] When I was illustrating the *Just so Stories*, I remembered and strove after that eye.'[8]

'How the Whale got his Throat' bases itself on American geography. When the Whale releases the Mariner on the beach of the Mariner's natal shore and the 'white-cliffs-of-Albion', the Whale calls out: 'Change here for Winchester, Ashuelot, Nashua, Keene, and stations on the *Fitch*burg Road', and 'just as he said "Fitch" the Mariner walked out of his mouth'.[9] The Fitchburg Railroad was a branch line which served Brattleboro, where the Kiplings lived. The Whale's cry contains an embedded joke which can only make sense in an American context because 'Winchester, Ashuelot' and so on were the names of railway stations in New Hampshire and Massachusetts in Kipling's time. It has to be added, though, that when this is explained the joke doesn't actually make *much* sense because the Whale has disgorged the Mariner on the English coast, not in New Hampshire or Massachusetts, and the white cliffs of Dover are not in any case part of the Mariner's 'natal-shore', given that he is Irish. The joke remains a riddle which is only partially unpacked.

How the *Just so Stories* Were Made

'How the Whale got his Throat' was first published in 1897 in *St Nicholas Magazine*, a prestigious and well-illustrated periodical for children edited by Mary Mapes Dodge (1831–1901). Kipling sent her the first three of the tales for this volume: the stories of the Whale, the Camel and the Rhinoceros. His initial plan was to stop there.

The first audience for the stories had been his eldest child, Josephine Kipling, known as 'Effie', and the 'Just so' of the title reflected the fact that Josephine was exacting. Kipling wrote and told many stories to his children which could be freely altered, but these bedtime stories were different: 'you were not allowed to alter those by a single little word. They had to be told just so; or Effie would wake up and put back the missing sentence. So at last they [the first group of stories] came to be like charms, all three of them, – the whale tale, the camel tale, and the rhinoceros tale.'*[10]

'How the Whale got his Throat' draws on the story of Jonah and the Whale, from the Book of Jonah (chapters 2 and 3) in the Old Testament, but Kipling also knew the version of the story given in a recently translated Islamic source of which he owned a set, the *'Rauzat-Us-Safa', or Garden of Purity* (1892).[12] He was also aware of an episode from *The Surprising Adventures of Baron Munchausen* (1785) in which the Baron is swallowed by a large fish and dances the horn-pipe until he is released. The late Victorian literary context to Kipling's talking animal stories includes popular illustrated editions for children of *Aesop's Fables* (e.g. *The Baby's Own Aesop*, illustrated by Walter Crane, 1887) as well as Lewis Carroll's Alice books (*Alice in Wonderland*, 1865, and *Through the Looking-Glass*, 1871) and Joel Chandler

---

* Angela Thirkell would later recall that when her family lived at North End House, Rottingdean, near Brighton, Kipling and his family, including her favourite cousin, Josephine, were living in a neighbouring house. 'The three Kipling children, Josephine, Elsie, and John were about the same ages as our nursery three. Josephine, very fair-haired and blue-eyed, was my bosom friend.' 'Cousin Ruddy', as she called Kipling, was a source of delight, and he would read the *Just so Stories* to the children. 'There was a ritual about them, each phrase having its special intonation which had to be exactly the same each time [...] there was an inimitable cadence, an emphasis of certain words, an exaggeration of certain phrases, a kind of intoning here and there which made his telling unforgettable.'[11]

Harris's *Uncle Remus* (1880) stories, which Kipling had read when he was a schoolboy. He would also have known the commercially successful children's books by Mrs Molesworth, which had high-quality illustrations. The best-known of these, *The Cuckoo Clock* (1877), tells the story of a little girl, Griselda, who is befriended by a magical cuckoo which emerges from the clock and is able to take her on adventures, including a journey to the far side of the moon. The plates, by Walter Crane, both carry the story forward and appeal to the imagination of a child audience.[13] Books for children from much earlier in the century included William Fordyce Mavor's educational books, *The English Spelling Book* (1819) and *First Book for Children* (1840).[14] Some of Mavor's images resemble Kipling's illustrations to his *Just so Stories*, especially those of a pleasingly robust elephant, a supercilious-looking camel and an elegant giraffe. Kipling also knew Margaret Gatty's sumptuously presented talking animal stories in *Parables from Nature: with Notes on the Natural History* (1888), which was illustrated by a premier league of artists including Kipling's 'Uncle Ned' together with Tenniel, Millais and Holman Hunt.[15]

With *The Jungle Book* (1894) and *The Second Jungle Book* (1895) Kipling had established himself as a leading contributor to the talking animal genre, and in his *Just so stories* he also offered playful alternatives to both the biblical story of creation in Genesis and the evolutionary narrative given by Darwin's *On the Origin of Species* (1859). There is also a bit of Lamarck thrown in for fun. The French naturalist Jean-Baptiste Lamarck (1744–1829) had seen change in species occurring because characteristics developed in one generation could be inherited by the next (his famous example was the giraffe's long neck developing as a result of reaching upwards for foliage).

Kipling's *Just so* illustrations remind us of his close connection with the Pre-Raphaelites. The most important of these connections was through his mother's sister, Georgiana Macdonald ('Aunt Georgie'), who had married Edward Burne-Jones in 1860. Burne-Jones, Kipling's beloved 'Uncle Ned', would become an important figure in Kipling's young life. During some school holidays when he was a boy at boarding school in Devon Kipling stayed with his mother's friends in London, 'three dear ladies who lived off the far end of Kensington High Street' in a house 'filled with books', which included Mrs Gatty's *Parables from Nature* with its lavish illustrations.[16] These ladies were Hannah Winnard and two cousins, Mary and Georgiana Craik. They were all literary, and Georgiana Craik was a prolific writer who published novels and children's books. Andrew Lycett refers to their house as an 'outpost of second-generation Pre-Raphaelitism', which clearly fed into the young Kipling's cultural and literary awakening.[17]

I want to step back from the *Just so Stories* themselves at this point to reflect on the immediate circumstances in which Kipling was writing his tales for small children. Why was Kipling living in Vermont in the 1890s? The answer to that question calls for a brief account of Kipling's early life up to the period between October 1882, when he started out as a journalist in India with the *Civil and Military Gazette*, and 1892, by which time he was settled in the United States with an American wife. Kipling was born in Bombay in 1865. His father, John Lockwood Kipling (known always to his friends and family as 'Lockwood'), had arrived in India in the previous year to make his career in the Indian education service, teaching at the Bombay School of Art. He was well liked, competent and successful, and his career in India prospered: in 1875 he was appointed principal of the new Mayo School of Art at Lahore in the Punjab, and curator of the Lahore museum.

As was the practice of middle-class English families settled in India, the Kiplings sent their children 'home' to the mother country for their education. Kipling and his younger sister were boarded out with strangers, Captain and Mrs Holloway, in what Kipling would later call 'the House of Desolation' at Southsea. They were left there in 1871 when they were still very young indeed (5 and 3 years old respectively). His childhood years in Southsea did severe and lasting psychological damage to Kipling. His experiences there are documented in his autobiography and in a searing short story, 'Baa Baa, Black Sheep' (1890). The Holloways were borderline shabby-genteel. Captain Pryse Holloway was a decent man who took a friendly interest in young Rudyard Kipling, but he had liver cancer and in 1874 he died. From this point onwards the child Kipling was at the mercy of the Captain's wife, Sarah Holloway. She struggled financially after her husband's death, and clearly resented the fact that little Rudyard had better prospects than her own 12-year-old son, Henry. When he wrote his autobiography Kipling claimed that she seized on his natural boisterousness as a pretext for giving him regular beatings.

In Kipling's 'Baa Baa, Black Sheep', the wretchedness of the little boy, Punch, at the hands of 'Aunty Rosa' reflects Kipling's memory of Mrs Holloway's house. The hated woman guardian appears again as the bullying 'Mrs Jennett' in his flawed but vividly written first novel, *The Light that Failed* (1891). Her final appearance in Kipling's writing is as a sadist named only as 'the Woman' in his posthumously published memoir, *Something of Myself* (1937). It is not clear to what extent the ill-treatment in this memoir is based on true memories. The incident in *Something of Myself* in which the child Kipling was made to wear a placard reading 'liar' on his way to school looks like a direct borrowing from *David Copperfield* (1849–50) (though his sister Alice, known as 'Trix', would claim that this particular piece of bullying did actually take place; it is possible that reading *Copperfield* gave Mrs Holloway the idea for this form of humiliation). The bullying was restricted to Kipling himself; his sister got on well with Mrs Holloway, and stayed in the house in Southsea for three years after Kipling himself had moved on. He was a self-willed child and it is likely that he got across Mrs Holloway and was punished, though his account of the bullying could also be in part a projection of unacknowledged anger with his own mother for leaving him with strangers.

In *Something of Myself* Kipling sought to retrieve some profit from this period of childhood wretchedness. He wrote there that living with Mrs Holloway in the 'House of Desolation' was not 'an unsuitable preparation for my future, in that it demanded constant wariness, the habit of observation, and attendance upon moods and tempers'.[18] He also claimed in the memoir that his sufferings there 'drained me of any capacity for real, personal hate for the rest of my days'.[19] This is contradicted by the version given in his story 'Baa Baa, Black Sheep', where he wrote 'when young lips have drunk deep of the bitter waters of Hate, Suspicion, and Despair, all the Love in the world will not wholly take away that knowledge'.*[20]

Lockwood Kipling's career in India brought him to a knowledge of, and sympathy with, Indian craftsmanship which was second to none, and when Rudyard Kipling had become an adult his creative life would be richly supported by his father's expertise. The image of a wood carver in Lahore epitomises Lockwood Kipling's respect for Indian craftsmanship.

From 1878 to 1882 Kipling was educated in England as a boarding pupil at the United Services College at Westward Ho!, Devon (the source for Kipling's stories in *Stalky & Co.*, 1899), a school which had the double attraction of being moderately cheap and having a family friend, Cormell Price, as its headmaster. The United Services College existed to train officers, but Kipling's poor eyesight barred him from a career in the services, and his parents' modest income could not enable him to go to a university. Cormell Price pointed him in the direction of journalism by making him editor of the school's journal, *The United Services Chronicle*. This led, through Lockwood Kipling's connections in Lahore, to Rudyard Kipling's first job as a professional writer, working with Stephen Wheeler, editor of Lahore's *Civil and Military Gazette*. During a period of leave in England (Easter 1882), Wheeler had got to know the young Kipling and was impressed enough to take him on. Thus, when Kipling left the United

---

* The influential critic Edward Said saw the bullying in Southsea as an experience which 'furnished Kipling with an enduring subject matter, the interaction between youth and unpleasant authority, which he rendered with great complexity and ambivalence throughout his life'.[21]

'A Wood Carver' by John Lockwood Kipling

Services College in July 1882 he was already assured of a job as a journalist in India.

On 20 September 1882 Kipling embarked on a passage back to India, his birthplace, which he had not seen since 1871 when as a small child he had been taken to be educated in England. On 18 October 1882 he disembarked at Bombay. He was a very mature adolescent: not yet

17 years old, he looked as though he was in his early twenties. His first biographer, Lord Birkenhead, wrote that he wore side-whiskers, 'which were at once prudently removed at the earnest entreaty of his mother'.[22] He travelled on from Bombay by train, and after four days arrived in Lahore and was reunited with his parents, of whom he had seen very little since his sixth year. He began working with the *Civil and Military Gazette* in October 1882. He very soon began to publish poems and stories in the *Civil and Military*, in addition to his reports on the lives and work of the British in India.

When he returned to India as a young adult the place which had been part of his identity as a small child was now experienced as both intimately known and startlingly fresh, and he was wide-eyed with excitement. He was a ravenous observer of the world that was now open to him, and he brought to it a double perception. The exotic and the marvellous, which he had known as a child, were extended for the young adult Kipling by his sense of the humming and tumultuous life of the place. But while the colour, liveliness and exoticism of the native quarters of Lahore enchanted him, much of British India bored him. 'In his heart,' as Birkenhead says, 'he probably despised many of the beefy conventional men who surrounded him, the army officers with their polo and gymkhanas and provincial flirtations, and the Government officials who were inclined to look down upon him as a mere journalist, and to shake their heads over his explorations in the back alleys and dim-lit temples of the bazaar.'[23]

As a journalist in India he worked very hard, and successfully, though at considerable personal cost. His mental health suffered, especially during the summer of 1884 when his parents and sister took refuge from the heat in a hill town called Dalhousie (less expensive than fashionable Simla), leaving him alone in the family bungalow in Lahore. He experimented with 'Indian hemp' (marijuana) and with a medication called Chlorodyne for the treatment of his 'night terrors'. A piece that he published in the *Civil and Military Gazette* reflects these experiences; the narrator is 'utterly alone on the verge of a waste of moonlit sand, stretching away to the horizon'.

Mountains swallow him and a river seeks to drown him; the episode ends with a nightmare rail journey relieved only when the narrator wakes.[24]

During the summer of 1888, when he was working in Allahabad, it became clear to him that this arena was not big enough for his ambitions. He wearied of Allahabad as a place, and when he returned to Lahore, the historic city in which he had first tasted success, he experienced that also as stale and exhausted: 'I have returned to the old, wearying, Godless futile life at a club – same men, same talk, same billiards – all *connu* and triply *connu*.'[25] In 1889 he took the firm decision to leave India and return to England, with a view to cashing in on his developing reputation as a writer.

This long voyage to England was made in the company of two friends, Alec and Edmonia Hill (Alec Hill was an Ulsterman who held an academic position in India, and his wife Edmonia, who would become a very valuable friend to Kipling, was an American). The tone of Kipling's travel narratives can often be boastful, with an implied claim that he has been everywhere and seen everything, but discovering Japan and Burma on this long sea-voyage showed him how little he actually knew. The enchantment of Burma would yield 'Mandalay' (1890), a ballad which became a famous music hall song. This journey included a prolonged exploration of the United States, the country which he would soon make his home.*

By October 1889 Kipling was in London and found himself taken up by the London literati and in particular by Andrew Lang, a genial and very influential figure who championed Kipling's stories set in India and

---

* Kipling's enthusiasm for the United States was never unqualified. In a letter to W.E. Henley he referred to the 'moral dry rot' that he found in America. There was 'no law that need be obeyed: no line to toe: no trace to kick over and no compulsion to do anything.' 'By consequence, a certain defect runs through everything – workmanship, roads, bridges, contracts, barter and sale and so forth – all inaccurate, all slovenly, all out of plumb and untrue.' The whole country is 'barbarism', Kipling declares, though barbarism 'plus telephone, electric light, rail and suffrage but all the more terrible for that reason'. In the same letter, though, he wrote 'I like it.'[26] This 'barbaric' country clearly stirred and excited him.

helped him to be elected a member of the Savile Club. Through such propitious introductions Kipling rapidly became part of a bustling London literary milieu. In the spring of 1890 he became a friend of Wolcott Balestier, an ambitious young American writer and literary agent based in London. This friendship would determine the future direction of Kipling's life.

What was the nature of this friendship? It seems to me certain that Angus Wilson was right to say that Kipling was 'much in love' with Wolcott,[27] although Kipling himself would not have been able to express his feeling as simply as that. In this context Philip Mason points to 'the platonic male affection that played so large a part in their [the Victorians'] society': 'Schoolmasters, dons, army officers, who devoted their lives to looking after young men, were at the heart of Victorian greatness; their charges were the loves of their lives.'[28] Philip Mason also suggests that Kipling's strong feeling for Balestier was a reaction from a previous loss. He had imagined himself in love with a self-centred woman artist called Flo Garrard (who appears as the unsympathetic 'Maisie' in his novel *The Light that Failed*). Mason writes: 'Sore from Flo Garrard's rejection, he felt himself thrown back on men for an affection that was safe, warm and intelligible.' And into this mood, as Mason puts it, 'was suddenly projected a young man who carried with him an atmosphere of intellectual and animal magnetism'.[29] So persuasive was Wolcott that Kipling agreed to collaborate with him on a work of fiction, *The Naulahka*, written by them jointly and published in 1892.

The friendship ended in sudden tragedy. In December 1891 Kipling was visiting his parents in Lahore on the eve of the Christmas holiday when he received news of Wolcott's sudden death (from typhoid, in Dresden) earlier in the month. Kipling had by this time got to know the whole Balestier family well, and had in particular formed a relationship with the elder of Wolcott's two sisters, Caroline ('Carrie'). The news of Wolcott's death reached Kipling in a telegram from Carrie which read: WOLCOTT DEAD STOP COME BACK TO ME STOP. Not pausing to celebrate Christmas with his own family in Lahore, Kipling immediately set sail for England. He arrived on 10 January 1892, disembarked, and was greeted by Carrie Balestier and her mother. He and Carrie were married on the 18th. This development was unwelcome to Kipling's parents and astonished some of his friends.[30] Henry James, always a loyal friend of Kipling, gave the bride away, but he had grave doubts about the match. He wrote to his brother, the philosopher William James, to say that Carrie was a 'hard devoted capable little person whom I don't in the least understand him marrying'. 'It's a union of which I don't forecast the future,' he added, 'though I gave her away at the altar in a dreary little wedding.' He clearly thought that Kipling had thrown himself away on a dull wife: 'Kipling strikes me personally as the most complete man of genius (as distinct from fine intelligence) that I have ever known.'[31] Henry James was wrong about the Kiplings' marriage: Carrie proved a strong and loyal partner throughout the years of a shared life which would encounter sharp and at times agonising reversals.

As a newly married couple the Kiplings settled in the Balestiers' home state, Vermont, in Bliss Cottage, which they rented from Carrie's mother. Literary friends back in England worried that Kipling was in danger of losing his audience and damaging his market by moving away from London while he was still a new and hot property. He wrote to reassure W.E. Henley – the editor of the *Scots Observer*, who had done more than anyone else to bring Kipling's work to a London audience – that he had made the right decision:

> Never you mind about my living in America. If you saw this life of ours and didn't happen to know your geography, it would be Africa, or Australia or another planet. I have what I need. Sunshine and the real earth within the reach of my hand, whenever I tire of messing with ink. Good stuff will come out of this in God's time which is not my time; and if nothing comes then I shall have led a sane clean life at least, and found new experiences.[32]

On 29 December of that first year in Vermont, his and Carrie's first child, Josephine Kipling, was born. It is a striking feature of this decade, 1892–1902, that the imaginative world explored in Kipling's writing is often one in which children and their experiences are in the foreground. In these ten years he invented the powerful mythical figure of Mowgli (in *The Jungle Book* and *The Second Jungle Book*),[33] and he wrote about the maturing of a spoilt American boy in *Captains Courageous* (1897) and the adventures of a group of schoolboys in *Stalky & Co* (1899). He conceived the *Just so Stories* soon after the birth of Josephine, wrote them episodically, and collected them for publication in 1902. In 1901 he published his masterpiece, *Kim*, his magnificent exploration of India from the perspective of a streetwise boy, the orphaned son of an Irish soldier.

Bliss Cottage was wholly unsuitable for a young married couple starting a family, and shortly after they settled in Vermont the Kiplings were involved in financial transactions with Carrie's brother, Beatty

Naulakha, Brattleboro, the Kiplings' American home, 1893–6

Balestier, to purchase 11.5 acres of his land on which they would build a house for themselves. They commissioned a big, practical and sturdy building which stood on a prominent site close to the various Balestier properties. The house was called Naulakha, in memory of Carrie's brother and Kipling's friend, Wolcott Balestier, with whom Kipling had collaborated on the novel of that name. Confusingly, the novel's title is *The Naulahka* – not a variant spelling, just an error, and almost certainly Wolcott's; it is a mark of Kipling's feeling for his dead brother-in-law that the title was never corrected. The Kiplings put up with the discomforts of Bliss Cottage until the big house was ready for them to move into, in the summer of 1893.

Becoming a married man and the father of a family, together with his decision to adopt his wife's country and settle in Vermont, decisively changed the direction of Kipling's work. The publications that had brought him fame as a very young man in 1890 (*Plain Tales from the Hills* and *Barrack-Room Ballads*) had been about the adult world of the British in India, the world in which his father had made his career. During his year in London, 1889–90, Kipling had registered sudden disgust with the affectations of some of the literary figures with whom he was then keeping company:

I consort with long-haired things
In velvet collar-rolls,
Who talk about the Aims of Art,
And 'theories' and 'goals',
And moo and coo with women-folk
About their blessed souls.[34]

Rural Vermont was refreshingly different from this. Living there excited and stimulated Kipling. Throughout his life he tried and enjoyed many male roles, and the one he was playing as a young family man in Vermont was that of a pioneering American farmer. A further feature of the protean nature of his identity was the closeness with which he held on to (hugged, one may say) the father figures in his life. Cormell Price remained a second father, to whom Kipling sent intimate and personal letters. One of these letters, from 5 November 1895, sets out three deep sources of contentment: little Josephine and her doings, his big American house with its substantial land which needed cultivating, and his steady flow of good writing. Josephine was 'in great and riotous form – of that age which asks every conceivable question all the while'. Kipling himself relished the 'busy monotony' of country life, 'spreading dung and fattening swine and building stone walls'.[35] This is protean Kipling at his most engaging, trying out a new role and identity for himself as a small English child might try on an American cowboy's hat.

2

HOW THE CAMEL GOT HIS HUMP

Now this is the next tale, and it tells how the Camel got his big hump. In
the beginning of years, when the world was so new-and-all, and the
Animals were just beginning to work for Man, there was a Camel, and
he lived in the middle of a Howling Desert because he did not want to
work; and besides, he was a Howler himself. So he ate sticks and thorns
and tamarisks and milkweed and prickles, most 'scruciating idle; and
when anybody spoke to him he said 'Humph!' Just 'Humph!' and no
more. Presently the Horse came to him on Monday morning, with a
saddle on his back and a bit in his mouth, and said, 'Camel, O Camel,
come out and trot like the rest of us.' 'Humph!' said the Camel; and the
Horse went away and told the Man. Presently the Dog came to him, with
a stick in his mouth, and said, 'Camel, O Camel, come and fetch and
carry like the rest of us.' 'Humph!' said the Camel; and the Dog went
away and told the Man. Presently the Ox came to him, with the yoke on
his neck, and said 'Camel, O Camel, come and plough like the rest of us.'
'Humph!' said the Camel; and the Ox went away and told the Man.[1]

The sense of 'he was a Howler himself' is somewhat obscure in the
published text. The manuscript of 'How the Camel got his Hump' makes
the point clearer. The relevant passage reads:

Once upon a time there was a Camel and he was born in the middle
of a howling desert, and he disliked it because there was nothing to

eat except sticks and stones and things so he sat down and howled too. And presently a Djinn came walking in a cloud of dust (Djinns always walk that way when they are at home). And the Djinn said 'Camel, oh Camel! Why do you make such a noise for nothing?' And the Camel said 'Djinn! Oh Djinn! I've been born in a howling desert.' And the Djinn said 'Let it Howl. It howled long before you were born and will go on howling long after you are grown up. Is there anything else that I can do for you today?'[2]

For the published story Kipling changed the focus so that the Camel's problem is no longer simple hunger; what now needs to be corrected in the Camel is his laziness.

Kipling's design for the initial capital N of the story ('Now this is the next tale') is ingeniously made of the camel's harness on a lateral view of the animal. Kipling signals that he is still parodying the creation myth ('when the world was so new-and-all') and in the case of the Camel's 'Humph!' he has added an additional twist in the form of wordplay. 'Humph' turns out to have three distinct senses: it is an expression of contempt, a physical feature of camels, and a verb. The three conscientious

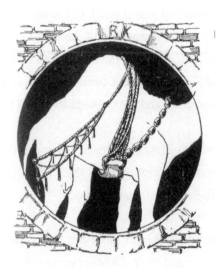

and hard-working animals resort to the form of village democracy that was familiar to Kipling from his early experience of India: 'They held a palaver, and an *indaba*, and a *punchayet*, and a pow-wow on the edge of the Desert; and the Camel came chewing milkweed *most* 'scruciating idle, and laughed at them. Then he said "Humph!" and went away again.'[3]

In the published text of the Camel story 'the Djinn in charge of All Deserts' arrives 'rolling in a cloud of dust (Djinns always travel that way because it is Magic)'. 'Rolling' in the cloud of dust is more inventive and expressive than the 'walking' of the manuscript. The Horse, the Dog and the Ox complain to the Djinn about the Camel: he won't trot, he won't fetch and carry, he won't plough, and he says 'Humph!' The Camel's 'Humph!' is transformed by the Djinn into a verb.

> 'Very good,' said the Djinn. 'I'll humph him if you will kindly wait a minute.' The Djinn rolled himself up in his dust-cloak, and took a bearing across the desert, and found the Camel most 'scruciatingly idle, looking at his own reflection in a pool of water.[4]

The punishment of the Camel when he is 'humphed' is so hedged about with magic and poetic invention that it does not feel like punishment at all. And this surely is a key point. One of a father's duties is to correct his children, but Kipling the story-teller steers away from Kipling the authority figure so that in his *Just so Stories* he is above all *playing* with his children, and playing with language, image and poetic usage. The children are invited to join him in his game as both charmed audience and delighted equals.

> 'My long and bubbling friend,' said the Djinn, 'what's this I hear of your doing no work, with the world so new-and-all?'
> 'Humph!' said the Camel.[5]

The Djinn then sits to make a Great Magic, a process carefully described in Kipling's caption to his picture illustrating this. The caption begins:

'This is the picture of the Djinn making the beginnings of the Magic that brought the Humph to the Camel. First he drew a line in the air with his finger, and it became solid, and then he made a cloud, and then he made an egg – you can see them at the bottom of the picture – and then there was a magic pumpkin which turned into a big white flame.' (The egg would have required a good deal of explanation to small children: the World Egg is associated with the moment of creation in Egyptian, Hindu and other ancient cultures.) As a result of the Great Magic the Djinn guides a Humph, or hump, out of a cloud ready to attach itself to the Camel's back if needed. The Camel unwisely says 'Humph!' once more, 'but no sooner had he said it than he saw his back, that he was so proud of, puffing up and puffing up into a great big lolloping humph'.[6] The caption insists that this 'punishment' of the Camel is gentle and generous, the mildest form of moral correction: 'It was a good Magic and a very

kind Magic really, though it had to give the Camel a Humph because the Camel was lazy. The Djinn in charge of All Deserts was one of the nicest of the Djinns, so he would never do anything really unkind.'[7]

The Djinn's magic takes effect: 'Here is the picture of the Djinn in charge of All Deserts guiding the Magic with his magic fan. The Camel is eating a twig of acacia, and he has just finished saying "Humph!" once too often.' The magic carries the Humph (the word is obviously now a noun) to be placed on the Camel's back.[8] As with his use of the story of Jonah and the Whale, Kipling is still keeping close to the notion of rewriting the biblical creation myth. The small lower image here is taken from part of the creation story. It includes Noah's Ark, lodged on a mountain following the flood. Kipling is clearly imitating the shape of a predella, or painted border, at the base of an altarpiece in medieval and renaissance art. (The word 'ark' was a rebus for Kipling's initials, R.K.) Josephine owned a Noah's Ark which had been given to her when she was 2 years old by her great-aunt Louisa Baldwin, in 1894. It had a fine and substantial collection of model animals; Kipling wrote that there were 'a hundred and twenty six' of them, all varnished for Josephine by his father Lockwood Kipling, to ensure that a small child could not poison herself by sucking the paint off the toy animals.[9]

Animals, especially the horse, the elephant and the camel, played key roles in the colonisation of India by the British. Given that none of the technology of modern warfare (tanks, fighter planes, aerial bombing, armed missiles and the like) had been thought of when the British were colonising India, animals played key roles on the battlefield. Camels were deployed by the British Army to carry weapons and baggage, and were a familiar and reassuring sight for an English boy who had been born in India. In chapter 10 of *Beast and Man in India* (1894) Lockwood Kipling described in detail the camel gun, a small and effective piece of ordnance mounted on the camel's hump by a technique developed by the Persians and adopted by the British.[10]

Kipling referred in a letter to a 'camel tale' as early as 1892, and his knowledge of camels goes back to his earliest years as a child in India. Soldiers serving in the British Army in India used camels as baggage animals, and found them obstinate beasts to manage. The soldiers adopted the Hindustani 'oont' as their term for the camel; 'Oonts' is the title of a poem in Kipling's *Barrack-Room Ballads*, published in

How the Camel got his Hump

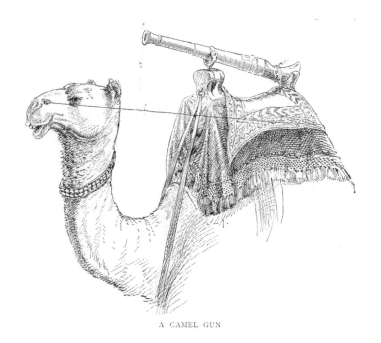

A CAMEL GUN

The camel in army service, with camel gun, by John Lockwood Kipling[11]

1890,* portraying the camel as an awkward creature, resistant to management, unlike the horse and the dog.

In the summer of 1893 Lockwood Kipling retired from his long service in India, and visited Rudyard and his family at Brattleboro. During that visit they jointly worked on Kipling's stories; they 'smoked over' the composition of the stories about Mowgli and his animal companions, and Lockwood made his illustrations for *The Second Jungle Book*. This was an exceptionally happy time in the relationship between Kipling and his father. Lockwood and Kipling worked together steadily, side by

---

* Fifteen of the *Barrack-Room Ballads* were first published in 1890 in *The Scots Observer*, edited by W.E. Henley. A collection was published in New York late in 1890 as *Departmental Ditties, Barrack-Room Ballads and Other Verses*; in March 1892 they were published in the UK as *Barrack-Room Ballads and Other Verses*. The twenty-one soldier poems in this volume were balanced by exactly the same number of 'Other Verses'.

side, Kipling writing his stories of Mowgli, the wolf pack and the talking animals in the jungle, while Lockwood made his sketches to illustrate the tales. Carrie and baby Josephine completed the picture of gentle harmony during that summer.

In the following year, 1894, Rudyard and Carrie Kipling spent much of the summer in England. The objectives of this visit were both to keep her English grandparents in touch with Josephine ('Baby Jo,' or 'Flat Curls', or 'Bips') and to enable Rudyard and Lockwood to continue collaborating. Kipling's parents, now settled in Tisbury, Wiltshire, had taken a house for the younger Kiplings for the duration of their stay.

Kipling worked very fast during this visit. His father's company spurred him on. He worked on three of the stories which would appear in *The Second Jungle Book*, and he completed a group of poems; he also established the plan for the *Just so Stories* and wrote a draft of 'How the Camel got his Hump'.[12] Reviewers had hailed him as a brilliant new young writer, and he made time to cash in on this growing reputation by catching up with literary acquaintances in London.*[13]

After completing his draft of the Camel story Kipling added to it a verse which is clearly about depression. Something about the Camel's personality, its arrogance and aloofness, may have stirred in Kipling memories of a blocked and depressed state he had suffered back in 1890 when he had been in good physical health but quite unable to work. Despite the pleasure offered by its linguistic inventiveness and Kipling's lovingly complex images, the Camel story ends with a poem which eschews complexity. Instead it offers a bracing and direct solution to the problem of depression:

---

* Back in Vermont, though, clouds were gathering. The Kiplings were becoming unpopular among their neighbours. Part of the problem was that Carrie was perceived as seeking to live with a degree of gentility and style which contrasted sharply with the plain and direct manners of the farming communities around them.[14]

How the Camel got his Hump

The camel's hump is an ugly lump
Which well you may see at the Zoo;
But uglier yet is the hump we get
From having too little to do.

Kiddies and grown-ups too-oo-oo,
If we haven't enough to do-oo-oo,
   We get the hump –
   Camelious hump –
The hump that is black and blue!

The remedy, it appears, is fresh air, exercise and working up a bit of a sweat:

The cure for this ill is not to sit still,
Or frowst with a book by the fire;
But to take a large hoe and a shovel also,
And dig till you gently perspire;

And then you will find that the sun and the wind,
And the Djinn of the Garden too,
   Have lifted the hump –
   The horrible hump –
The hump that is black and blue![15]

This is written in denial of Kipling's own experience. His own low states of mind were not staved off by exercise and vigorous activity. Symptoms of depression show in some of his earliest work – in a short piece called 'De Profundis', for example, written in 1881, and an account of desperate insomnia called 'Till the Day Break', first published in 1888.[16] When he sailed from India to England in 1889 he suffered from severe depression (expressed in his many letters to Edmonia Hill). He drew on his personal experience of depression in some of his strongest mature stories. 'The House Surgeon', published in *Actions and Reactions* in 1909, is based on Kipling's memory of a 'hump' that he suffered while staying in Rock House, a rented house at St Marychurch near Torquay, in 1896–7. He and his family had just returned to England from Vermont, in unhappy circumstances, and it may be that Kipling externalised his inner unease here to a point where the house itself seemed to have an illness. On the face of it, Rock House had everything to commend it. It was 'large and bright, with big rooms each and all open to the sun, the grounds embellished with great trees and the warm land dropping southerly to the clean sea under the Mary Church cliffs'. But, as Birkenhead wrote, the place gave him 'a malaise of soul' which he described as a 'gathering blackness of mind and sorrow of the heart'. It seemed to Kipling that it was the '*Feng-Shui* – the spirit of the house itself – that quenched the sunshine and fell upon them every time they entered it, freezing the very words upon their lips'.[17]

In 'The House Surgeon' this malaise of the soul is vividly expressed. 'A little grey shadow, as it might have been a snowflake seen against the light,' heralds for the narrator a crisis in which 'my amazed and angry soul dropped, gulf by gulf, into the Horror of great darkness which is spoken of in the Bible'.[18] The force of this story persuades me both that Kipling was drawing on personal experience, and that his mental distress during 1890 included a crisis like this one. Kipling's collection called *Life's Handicap* (1891) contains some stories which again seem to have drawn on his own troubled states of mind. In 'At the End of the Passage', a young English engineer named Hummil dies of sheer terror (related to his recurrent waking nightmare of 'A blind face that cried and can't wipe its eyes, a blind face that chases him down corridors'). Hummil is thrown off balance not just by heat but also by an unnamed horror, which may well reflect the night terrors that overtook Kipling in Lahore. In a related tale, 'The Mark of the Beast', a big cheerful Englishman called Fleete insults a group of worshippers of the god Hanuman by stubbing out his cigar on the brow of the god's effigy. He is cursed by a 'silver man' (a leper) who lives in Hanuman's temple, and as a result of the curse he becomes a werewolf. A macabre (and nauseating) detail of the story here is that the curse is lifted only when Fleete's English companions torture the leper with heated gun-barrels.[19]

Such a tale seems worlds away from the playfulness of the *Just so Stories*, yet there is an intriguing small link. The 'mark' in 'The Mark of the Beast' is the pattern on a leopard's hide; where the leper has touched Fleete his flesh has become discoloured: 'Fleete open his shirt and showed us, just over his left breast, a mark, the perfect double of the black rosettes – the five or six irregular blotches arranged in a circle – on a leopard's hide.'[20] In 'How the Leopard got his Spots' the Leopard is an eager ingénu, guided by his wiser friend the Ethiopian. There is wordplay here in 'leper–leopard', and the physical transformations displayed in the first seven *Just so Stories* are finding a nightmare equivalent here in Kipling's mind.

'The hump that is black and blue', then, was part of Kipling's young manhood. His relentless travelling and abrupt emotional changes of direction belong to a pattern of behaviour which signals serious mental disturbance. His parents' company in 1890 helped him through his nervous breakdowns by bringing back memories of his early childhood in India. That had been a time of enchantment. The child Kipling spoke Hindi more easily than he spoke English, and the happy recollection of stories told to him by gentle Indian servants when he was very small underlies some of the delight that he takes in telling his *Just so* stories. English children in India had an afternoon sleep in the heat of the Indian day, and his Goanese *ayah* (or nursemaid) and Meeta, his Hindu 'bearer', would settle the two Kipling children, Rudyard and Trix, by 'tell[ing] us stories and Indian nursery songs all unforgotten, and we were sent into the dining-room after we had been dressed, with the caution "Speak English now to Papa and Mama." So one spoke "English," haltingly translated out of the vernacular idiom that one thought and dreamed in.'[21]

Kipling liked to speak of the 'family square' as a close-knit unit of four people living in harmony, first in Bombay and subsequently in Lahore. This was actually a fiction, I think, a compensatory invention written in denial of his anger with his parents for abandoning him in Southsea when he was an infant. The 'square' comprised Alice, his lively and pretty mother; Trix, his sister; Lockwood, his father; and Rudyard himself. His perception of the family square was rose-tinted: his parents' marriage had its problems. Alice Kipling was older than her husband and much more sociable and lively than he was. She attracted many of the British men working in India, both in Lahore and in Simla. She showed signs of becoming jealous of her daughter as Trix matured into a young beauty. Older men, some of them with dangerous reputations, made a point of paying court to Trix, and she seems to have enjoyed their attention.

Lockwood Kipling's *Beast and Man in India* had given a decidedly noble version of the camel story, where the hump is a mark of honour. On the death of an Islamic ruler his corpse was laid on the back of a camel which was sent out into the wilderness until the Angel Gabriel met him. The Angel 'gave him a hump like the mountain into which he disappeared, and feet to spread on the yielding sand'.[22] Kipling's camel story, where the hump is a penalty for idleness, reads as though it was conceived in friendly rivalry with his father's version.

The readership for children's books had grown steadily throughout the nineteenth century, and during Kipling's lifetime it had been transformed. Early in the century, writing for children had tended to be didactic and moralising, though at the same time popular 'nonsense' writing for children was garnering a market. In stories by William Roscoe and Sarah Martin, animals perform human actions. In Roscoe's *The Butterfly Ball and the Grasshopper's Feast* (1806) the creatures perform a tightrope dance, and in Sarah Martin's *The Adventures of Old Mother Hubbard and her Dog* (1805) the dog smokes a pipe, plays the flute, rides a goat and reads the news. Part of the fun is that the animals do not lose their animal characteristics.[23] Obviously Lewis Carroll's *Alice* books are also 'nonsense'

Father and son in partnership: Lockwood and Rudyard Kipling in the 1890s

stories, though with the crucial distinction that they firmly endorse control in the form of logic. In *Alice in Wonderland* the 7-year-old Alice's sharp perception of loose and muddled thinking and behaviour in the humans and animals she encounters lends her authority throughout the text. In the courtroom scene the King of Hearts tries to banish Alice by reading out 'Rule forty-two': '*All persons more than a mile high to leave the court*'. Alice protests. The King defends the rule as 'the oldest rule in the book' and Alice confounds him by saying 'then it ought to be Number One'.[24] 'Rules', as understood by adults, are subverted in the *Alice* books and Kipling's *Just so Stories*, especially in the first three in which the

Whale, the Camel and the Rhinoceros incur mild and playful penalties for their behaviour.

Real and severe punishment for misbehaviour among children was part of the code of the British public schools, which saw massive growth in numbers and popularity in the latter part of the nineteenth century. This pattern, including many instances of corporal punishment for adolescent boys, is insisted upon in the stories of school life in *Stalky & Co.* Kipling dedicated this book to his former headmaster, Cormell Price, and the dedication is immediately followed by verses equating 'love' of boys with violent punishment of them. The row of buildings in which the United Services College was housed is identified here as 'Twelve bleak houses by the shore!':

Western wind and open surge
Took us from our mothers;
Flung us on a naked shore
(Twelve bleak houses by the shore!
Seven summers by the shore!)
'Mid two hundred brothers.

There we met with famous men
Set in office o'er us;
And they beat on us with rods –
Faithfully with many rods –
Daily beat us on with rods,
For the love they bore us.[25]

The young men emerging from schools like the United Services College were needed to administer and control Britain's overseas possessions, especially India, and it was seen as appropriate that their training should be rigorous. The most famous of Kipling's talking animals in the *Just so Stories*, the Elephant's Child, has a training which is similarly rigorous in the sense that he is regularly spanked for his ' 'satiable curtiosity'. Beyond that, though, there is very little connection in terms of setting, mood, tone and dramatic organisation between the *Just so Stories* and *Stalky & Co.*, yet they are close to each other in date of publication. A radically different part of Kipling's mind had created *Stalky & Co.*

3

HOW THE RHINOCEROS
GOT HIS SKIN

ONCE upon a time, on an uninhabited island on the shores of the
Red Sea, there lived a Parsee from whose hat the rays of the sun were
reflected in more-than-oriental splendour.* And the Parsee lived by
the Red Sea with nothing but his hat and his knife and a cooking-
stove of the kind that you must particularly never touch. And one day
he took flour and water and currants and plums and sugar and things,
and made himself one cake which was two feet across and three feet
thick. It was indeed a Superior Comestible (*that's* Magic), and he put
it on the stove because *he* was allowed to cook on that stove, and he
baked it and he baked it till it was all done brown and smelt most
sentimental.[1]

The Parsee has cooked himself his cake, 'But just as he was going to eat it
there came down to the beach from the Altogether Uninhabited Interior
one Rhinoceros with a horn on his nose, two piggy eyes, and few manners.'
'One', 'two', 'few': the narrator's mock-pedantic sequence here alerts us to
a recurrent stylistic feature of the *Just so Stories*, the elegance and textual

---

* The Parsees worshipped light and fire, and therefore the sun was central to their
religious outlook. The Parsee is 'allowed' to cook on the oil-stove, while in any
middle-class English family a small child would be kept away from the kitchen for
fear of burning itself (and of annoying the cook). In 1895 Carrie Kipling had
suffered severe burns to her face when she opened the furnace which heated
Naulakha, and it may be that a memory of this has added to Kipling's caution
about stoves 'that you must particularly never touch'.

precision with which each story points up its own slightly unidiomatic usages. 'Sentimental' for the smell of a cake is an instance of synaesthesia, simultaneously clearly 'wrong' and delightfully right.

The Rhinoceros 'upset the oil-stove with his nose, and the cake rolled on the sand, and he spiked that cake on the horn of his nose, and he ate it, and he went away, waving his tail'. The narrative voice adapts itself to the child audience's delighted expectation. The title of the story in the British Library manuscript was 'Why the Rhinoceros's skin doesn't fit',[2] and the story pays close attention to the way the Rhinoceros's skin is attached to him. 'In those days the Rhinoceros's skin fitted him quite tight. There were no wrinkles in it anywhere.' He looked 'exactly like a Noah's Ark Rhinoceros', and 'had no manners then, and he has no manners now, and he never will have any manners'.[3] The Rhinoceros and the Parsee may have been suggested to Kipling by one of the stories in E. W. Lane's *Arabian Nights' Entertainment*, in which es-Sindibad (Sinbad the Sailor) is stranded on a desert island, and escapes from it by mounting a huge bird (the Arabic word for it is a *roc*) which flies him to an adventure in a remote place frequented by merchants but also inhabited by rhinoceroses.

In the next image the Parsee is indulging himself as the Rhinoceros looks on. The caption tells us that it is a picture 'of the Parsee beginning to eat his cake on the Uninhabited Island in the Red Sea on a very hot day; and of the Rhinoceros coming down from the Altogether Uninhabited Interior'. The Rhinoceros's skin in this image is still smooth 'with three buttons that button it up' (the buttons are 'underneath, so you can't see them'). 'The wheel-thing lying on the sand in front belonged to one of Pharaoh's chariots when he tried to cross the Red Sea.' We also learn that 'the Parsee's name was Pestonjee Bomonjee, and the Rhinoceros was called Strorks, because he breathed through his mouth instead of his nose'.[4]

Pestonjee Bomonjee was a real person, a Parsee who was one of Lockwood Kipling's students at the school of art in Bombay. This man later became a well-known artist. The founder of the Bombay School of Art, which employed Lockwood Kipling, was also a Parsee, famous and

venerated in India, called Sir Jamsetjee Jeejeebhoy. The names were in themselves exotic and appealing, and also it is likely that the Parsees caught Kipling's imagination both because of Sir Jamsetjee's wealth and benevolence and also because of their ancient lineage and particular faith. They were descendants of Persians who took refuge in India following the Arab invasion of Persia in the seventh and eighth centuries. They were followers of the sage Zoroaster, and worshipped God in the forms of light and fire.

The Rhinoceros story ends with a playful coda and a child's ballad. 'The Parsee came down from his palm-tree, wearing his hat, from which the rays of the sun were reflected in more-than-oriental splendour, packed up his cooking-stove, and went away in the direction of Orotavo, Amygdala, the Upland Meadows of Anantarivo, and the Marshes of Sonaput.'[5] None of these places exist, but they have hints of the names of real places: Sonapur is in India, Antananarivo is the capital of Madagascar, and Orotava is a port in Tenerife in the Canary Islands.

The wheel of Pharaoh's chariot is a reference to a key event in Jewish history. In Exodus 14 the people of Israel reproach Moses for his leadership, which has brought them to what seems like a barren impasse on the shore of the Red Sea:

And they said unto Moses, Because there were no graves in Egypt, hast thou taken us away to die in the wilderness? Wherefore hast thou dealt thus with us, to carry us forth out of Egypt?

Moses assures them of the 'salvation of the Lord'. A pillar of cloud passes between the camp of the Egyptians and the camp of Israel:

And Moses stretched out his hand by the sea; and the Lord caused the sea to go back by a strong east wind all that night, and made the sea dry land, and the waters were divided.

The Egyptians pursue the people of Israel, and with Moses' second gesture the sea returns:

And covered the chariots, and the horsemen, and all the host of Pharaoh that came into the sea after them; there remained not so much as one of them. (Exodus, 14, 11, 21, 28)

Kipling's ancient Egyptians had itemised their chariots as methodically as the British in India had itemised their cannon. The letters printed on the chariot wheel read 'ptian Army 17633'. (And Kipling's initials, R.K., appear under the Rhinoceros's foot.)[6]

The Egyptians had enslaved the people of Israel. Empire building and the subjugation of a great people had existed in the ancient world as robustly as they thrived in British India, and the image raises the then impermissible thought that the British Empire will in due course vanish as thoroughly as the Egyptian one had. There is a hint here of the symbolic force present in the 'vast and trunkless legs of stone' from Shelley's sonnet about a vanished empire, 'Ozymandias' (1817). 'Ozymandias' was the Greek name for the Pharaoh Ramses II, whose vanished power is signalled by the half-buried Egyptian chariot wheel. Shelley the passionate revolutionary is a surprising presence in a story by Kipling. Still, Kipling grasped the lessons of history clearly enough to know that all empires must pass (witness here his stories about the end of the Roman occupation of Britain in *Puck of Pook's Hill*).

The theft of the cake leads into the narrative of the Parsee's revenge, which can be seen as a miniature and personalised variant of the revenge inflicted on the Egyptians by the people of Israel. Three weeks (precisely specified) after the theft of the cake, in a heat wave, 'everybody took off all the clothes they had'. 'Everybody' suggests that a number of people are in on the action, though in fact the cast of the story is restricted to two figures, the Parsee and the Rhinoceros. 'The Parsee took off his hat; but the Rhinoceros took off his skin and carried it over his shoulder as he came down to the beach to bathe. In those days it buttoned underneath with three buttons and looked like a waterproof.' (Kipling's children would have known exactly how to visualise this from their own waterproofs.) The Parsee takes refuge in a tree to watch him from a safe distance. Then the Parsee finds the skin. There is further dead-pan comic pedantry here in the narrative voice's use of numbers. 'He smiled one smile that ran all round his face two times. Then he danced three

times round the skin.' He fills his hat with cake-crumbs, 'for the Parsee never ate anything but cake, and never swept out his camp'. He rubs the crumbs into the Rhinoceros's skin, 'just as full of old, dry, stale, tickly cake-crumbs and some burned currants as ever it could *possibly* hold'.[7]

The caption to the image tells us that: 'This is the Parsee Pestonjee Bomonjee sitting in his palm-tree and watching the Rhinoceros Strorks bathing near the beach of the Altogether Uninhabited Island after Strorks has taken off his skin. The Parsee has rubbed the cake-crumbs into the skin, and he is smiling to think how they will tickle Strorks when Strorks puts it on again.' The story gives plenty of space to the Rhinoceros's physical discomfort. He tries to scratch, to no effect:

> And then he lay down on the sands and rolled and rolled and rolled, and every time he rolled the cake-crumbs tickled him worse and worse and worse. Then he ran to the palm-tree and rubbed and rubbed and rubbed himself against it. He rubbed so much and so hard that he rubbed his skin into a great fold over his shoulders, and another fold underneath, where the buttons used to be (but he rubbed the buttons off), and he rubbed some more folds over his legs. And it spoiled his temper, but it didn't make the least difference to the cake-crumbs.[8]

The energy of passages like this has young audiences helpless with laughter. The central conceit is that the rhinoceros's deeply folded skin, and his bad temper, are punishments for greed. This story has another '*sloka*', clearly a feature that Kipling was fond of, and itself a didactic rhyme:

> Them that takes cakes
> Which the Parsee-man bakes
> Makes dreadful mistakes.[9]

How the Rhinoceros got his Skin

Kipling had originally planned just three creation tales for *St Nicholas Magazine*, and when first published in February 1898 this third tale came with a valedictory signal announcing it as the last of the stories: '*Now this is the last tale and it tells how the Rhinoceros got his wrinkly skin.*'* For the collected *Just so Stories* of 1902 he changed it. The 'Once upon a time' of the 1902 text declares that this traditional way of starting a story still has currency. The geography of the Rhinoceros's island is as fanciful, and as exact in its phrasing, as 'the land where the Bong-tree grows' in Lear's 'The Owl and the Pussycat' (1871), and the little ballad which closes the story continues the joke:

This Uninhabited Island

Is off Cape Gardafui,

By the Beaches of Socotra

And the Pink Arabian Sea:

But it's hot – too hot from Suez

For the likes of you and me

Ever to go

In a P. and O.

And call on the Cake-Parsee![10]

J.M.S. Tompkins writes illuminatingly about Kipling's stories for children. Her feeling for them is deep and personal: 'It is not easy to take a dispassionate view of a book to which we have been much indebted in youth. Sometimes we are even unwilling to disturb the original associations by trying to do so.' In her own case, as a child 'of the generation for which they were first written', she had the great advantage 'of being read aloud to,

---

* The Rhinoceros tale was the third and last of the *Just so Stories* to be published in *St Nicholas Magazine* where Kipling had also published the first stories about Mowgli, the Indian child reared by wolves. The story of Mowgli's adoption by the wolf family, 'Mowgli's Brothers', was published in *St Nicholas Magazine* in January 1894. The *Just so Stories* and the Mowgli stories were born in the same editorial cradle.

This photograph of Kipling on a sea passage from South Africa to England in 1902, reading the *Just so Stories* to a group of children, gives a sense of his ability to enchant his audience

extremely well, by both my parents'. In the *Just so Stories* she responded to the text's pleasing mystifications:

> I did not know what 'racial talks' were, or 'gay shell torques' which sounded the same, and no one bothered me by explaining; they sounded satisfactory when I repeated the lines or my mother sang them. But the great joy was the pictures, with their deeply satisfying detail. I used to work through Taffimai's necklace, checking the beads off by the list helpfully supplied by the author, though the black snake-like background always puzzled me.[11]

Tompkins never loses sight of the fact that the *Just so Stories* were written for *performance*. The reading aloud of a text and the performing of a text were features of Victorian writing which we now tend to overlook.

How the Rhinoceros got his Skin

Famously, Tennyson, with his majestic stature and his great mane of dark hair, was a formidably impressive reader of his own work. This is evidenced by the heroic organ-roll of his voice, with his Lincolnshire accent still noticeable in a recording made late in his life of him reading 'The Charge of the Light Brigade' (1854). (Sadly, his famous and oft-repeated readings of 'Maud' have to be imagined rather than experienced.) His physical presence was universally noted and admired: the beard, the Spanish hat and the flowing cape were parts of his public persona which signalled 'world-famous post-Romantic poet' wherever he went.

Kipling, equally famous, equally sought-out, was the physical opposite of Tennyson. At Bateman's, Kipling's house in Sussex, the National Trust has a black-and-white film from the 1930s of Kipling addressing a public audience; here we see a short man with thick spectacles, a reedy voice and an unfortunately hectoring mode of delivery. Yet we know that as a young man among the British residents at Simla Kipling was an effective performer in amateur theatricals, and we know that his readings of the *Just so Stories* enchanted his young audiences. The voice must have been graceful, playful, loving and mellifluous in ways which surviving recordings of him have failed to convey. The voice would also have offered successful characterisation of his talking animals. Did the Kangaroo speak with an Australian accent? Certainly the Crocodile in the story of the Elephant's Child would have spoken in deep, seductive tones.

The Rhinoceros tale has a decorative initial which seems to have little connection with the story: it belongs to South America, not to Africa. The image shows a stylised human figure wearing a bird costume which is derived from Mayan figurative art, and the animals to each side of it are jaguars. The Painted Jaguar and his mother are key characters in the seventh story, 'The Beginning of the Armadilloes', which is set on the 'turbid Amazon'. The details of this initial place it in pre-Columbian Mexico. The elongated figure above the bird-man's head is probably the plumed serpent Quetzalcoatl, and both the plumed serpent and the

jaguar were significant religious symbols for the Mayans. We can take the Mayan imagery as part of a linking narrative which is extraneous to the plots of any of the *Just so Stories*. Like the map of the Amazon in the Armadillo story, and also like some of the figures in the illustrations to the Tabu story, these images hint teasingly at a narrative sequence which exists outside, and in parallel with, the individual stories, and which links to both the alternative creation narratives and to the Stone Age man narratives in the volume.

It is impossible to make neat sense of the Mayan image here. We are looking at a riddle which is as unanswerable as the famous instance in *Alice in Wonderland* where Alice is asked 'Why is a raven like a writing desk?' (There is no answer.)[12] There is no explanation here of the Mexican figures in the story of the Rhinoceros. We have unrelated clues, questions and diverse imagery, and we, the readers, serve as the only point of connection. The stories need to be read slowly. The over-hasty reader can trip over the riddles, or ignore them, and thus lose some of the pleasure that Kipling has prepared for us.

How the Rhinoceros got his Skin

The Rhinoceros tale was the last of the *Just so Stories* to be conceived and told while the family were living in Vermont. By the end of 1896 Kipling's comfortable life at Naulakha, and his happiness as an Englishman who had adopted the American way of life, had been destroyed by a violent quarrel with Carrie Kipling's surviving brother. On first acquaintance, Beatty Balestier had seemed an embodiment of all that was strong and sturdy in American communities. Lord Birkenhead described him as 'no mere Vermont hayseed' but a cultivated man of 'devastating and unsimulated charm'. The charm coexisted with a strong ego: he was a man who 'intended to live his own life and would not tolerate advice or admonition – a life of hard manual work in hot sun or driving snow, broken by mad sleigh races with lathered horses across the frozen Connecticut River for wagers he could not afford, bouts of wild dissipation, and acts of neighbourly kindness'.[13] The Kiplings had become closely financially involved with Beatty as a consequence of employing him on their land at Naulakha. Sadly, though, misunderstandings had built up over such matters as payments and the extent of Beatty's rights over property which had previously belonged to him. Harry Ricketts points out that Carrie Kipling's diary shows 'what went wrong':

> It shows that from October 1892 to June 1895 she, as the accountant and paymaster of the 'Committee of Ways and Means', was handing out money to Beatty, often on a daily basis. These payments included his wages as foreman and money for materials and labour on the house. What was striking about almost all these sums was that they were so small, usually ranging between three and twenty-five dollars. In other words, no large sums, for fear that Beatty would blow them on drink.[14]

A man of Beatty's temperament was likely to resent the fact that he was under his sister's control and in his brother-in-law's pay. The tension between the big rangy improvident American and the small nervous wealthy Englishman built up to a point where Beatty threatened Kipling with violence (for supposedly spreading rumours about his, Beatty's, extravagance). Kipling unwisely took Beatty to court for threatening physical assault. The case was a technical victory for Kipling, but he was unprepared for the reaction to it among his fellow citizens in Vermont. Beatty was a well-liked member of a long-established Brattleboro family, and the community closed ranks against the Kiplings. There were lampoons in the local press. The *Brattleboro Reformer* used the metre and verse length of Kipling's 'Danny Deever' (1890) to mock him.

> 'What makes the Kipling breathe so hard?' said the copper ready-
> made.
> 'He's mighty scart, he's mighty scart', the First Selectman said.
> 'What makes his wife look down so glum?' said the copper
> ready-made.
> 'It's family pride, it's family pride', the First Selectman said.[15]

Taking Beatty to court had been a major error of judgement, and it made both the Kiplings ill. Carrie wrote in her diary for 12 May 1896: 'Rud a total wreck. Sleeps all the time, dull and listless and dreary. These are dark days for us.'[16] The tensions following the court case – with Beatty and his family still living in close proximity – were all too much for the Kiplings and they decided to leave Vermont and sail back to England. It was heart-breaking for them both. 'I love Naulakha,' Kipling said, with stark simplicity. Birkenhead, with his access to Carrie's diary as evidence, filled this out:

> As he spoke of the touch of autumn already on the distant hills, tears
> filled his eyes. He was leaving the only home he had known, through
> a farcical misunderstanding with a man who should have been his
> friend. Never in the years ahead was he to talk of Brattleboro, or read
> anything that reminded him of that dreadful year.[17]

How the Rhinoceros got his Skin

Was Beatty in some sense the Rhinoceros? He was strong, generous and impulsive, and the kind of man from one of the 'younger nations' with whom Kipling on his own would have been willing to make a good relationship. At the same time he was also thin-skinned and irritable. The Rhinoceros found the crumbs in his skin intolerable, and Beatty found what he believed to be the stories that his sister and her husband had been telling about him insufferably wounding. The breach would never be healed. Kipling and his family sailed to England and settled near his Burne-Jones relations in the coastal village of Rottingdean, Sussex. Kipling's son John was born at Rottingdean in 1897, and Kipling made his home there from 1897 to 1902.

4

HOW THE LEOPARD GOT HIS SPOTS

In the days when everybody started fair, Best Beloved, the Leopard lived in a place called the High Veldt. 'Member it wasn't the Low Veldt, or the Bush Veldt, or the Sour Veldt, but the 'sclusively bare, hot, shiny High Veldt, where there was sand and sandy-coloured rock and 'sclusively tufts of sandy-yellowish grass. The Giraffe and the Zebra and the Eland and the Koodoo and the Hartebeest lived there; and they were 'sclusively sandy-yellow-brownish all over; but the Leopard, he was the 'sclusivest sandiest-yellowish-brownest of them all – a greyish-yellowish catty-shaped kind of beast, and he matched the 'sclusively yellowish-greyish-brownish colour of the High Veldt to one hair. This was very bad for the Giraffe and the Zebra and the rest of them; for he would lie down by a 'sclusively yellowish-greyish-brownish stone or clump of grass, and when the Giraffe or the Zebra or the Eland or the Koodoo or the Bush-Buck or the Bonte-Buck came by he would surprise them out of their jumpsome lives. He would indeed![1]

In Kipling's 'Baa Baa, Black Sheep' the distinction between black and white races is raised. 'Black Sheep', the nickname given to the child Punch (Kipling) in the story, evokes both a morally culpable member of a group and a dark-skinned person. The school to which the child goes has a boy who is a *hubshi* (a pejorative colloquialism for a black African). This disparaging usage comes from Indians speaking in Hindi, and Kipling and his sister would have heard it from the Indian servants familiar to them in their childhood. Punch's recoil from a *hubshi* has been imprinted by the 'bearer' (manservant) and the '*ayah*' (nanny) of his infancy. Punch experiences the sharp horror of what would have been seen at the time as social degradation. There were 'two Jews and a negro [...] in the assembly. "That's a *hubshi*," said Black Sheep to himself. "Even Meeta [the name of Kipling's own bearer] used to laugh at a *hubshi*. I don't think this is a proper place." '[2] Punch's own nickname, Black Sheep, reinforces the continuum 'Black'–'*hubshi*'–'racial inferior'. (At the same time, though, to be a 'black sheep' is also to be the striking exception to the generality of a species. Punch is a bright child who asks sharp questions and challenges adult authority.)

In response to Aunty Rosa's 'How do you like school?' Punch is initially circumspect ('I think it is a very nice place') but her next move elicits his true opinion. 'I suppose you warned the boys of Black Sheep's character?' says Aunty Rosa to 'Harry' (her son, based directly on Mrs Holloway's son). ' "If I was with my father," said Black Sheep, stung to the quick, "I shouldn't *speak* to those boys. He wouldn't let me. They live in shops. I saw them go into shops – where their fathers live and sell things." '[3]

I introduce the racist reference to a *hubshi* here in order to bring out the very sharp contrast between this and the attitude to a black figure in 'How the Leopard got his Spots'. Kipling is in complete accord with his black Ethiopian. The title of 'How the Leopard got his Spots' refers to a warning to the people of Jerusalem in the Book of Jeremiah. The Jews have been neglecting their religious duties for some forty years and unless they change their ways God will punish them; their city of Jerusalem will be destroyed. 'Woe unto thee, O Jerusalem! Wilt thou not be made clean? When shall it once be?' There is moral hope for the Jews, though, in this question: 'Can the Ethiopian change his skin, or the leopard his spots? *then* may ye also do good, that are accustomed to do evil' (Jeremiah 13:23–25). Kipling redirects these phrases so that they refer not to moral iniquity but to adaptation and survival: Jeremiah is Darwinised. The Leopard has a companion, 'an Ethiopian with bows and arrows (a 'sclusively greyish-brownish-yellowish man he was then)', who lived on the High Veldt with the Leopard. The two used to hunt together – 'the Ethiopian with his bows and arrows, and the Leopard 'sclusively with his teeth and claws – till the Giraffe and the Eland and the Koodoo and the Quagga and all the rest of them didn't know which way to jump, Best Beloved. They didn't indeed!'[4] The animals on whom they normally prey develop survival skills:

> After a long time – things lived for ever so long in those days – they learned to avoid anything that looked like a Leopard or an Ethiopian; and bit by bit – the Giraffe began it, because his legs were the longest – they went away from the High Veldt. They scuttled for days and days and days till they came to a great forest, 'sclusively full of trees and bushes and stripy, speckly, patchy-blatchy shadows, and there they hid: and after another long time, what with standing half in the shade and half out of it, and what with the slippery-slidy shadows of the trees falling on them, the Giraffe grew blotchy, and the Zebra grew stripy, and the Eland and the Koodoo grew darker, with little wavy grey lines on their backs like bark on a tree trunk; and so, though you could hear them and smell them, you could very seldom see them, and then only when you knew precisely where to look. They had a beautiful time in the 'sclusively speckly-spickly shadows of the forest, while the Leopard and the Ethiopian ran about over the 'sclusively greyish-yellowish-reddish High Veldt outside, wondering where all their breakfasts and their dinners and their teas had gone. At last they were so hungry that they ate rats and beetles and rock-rabbits, the Leopard and the Ethiopian, and then they had the Big Tummy-ache, both together.[5]

The desperation to which they are reduced could well have been drawn from Kipling's knowledge of famines in the recent history of British India. The most widely reported of these disasters was the so-called Great Famine of 1876–8. This was caused initially by drought and crop failure, but had been exacerbated by the behaviour of the then Governor-General of India, Lord Lytton (son of Bulwer Lytton, the celebrated fashionable novelist). Lytton took the view that good economic management justified the *export* of Indian grain during this period. His intentions were in part benevolent. Nevertheless it was on his watch that over a period of two years much of central and southern India suffered 'catastrophic hunger and death'; it is estimated there were 5 million victims of this famine.[6]

The Leopard and his friend are relieved from their hunger by a Creature called the Baviaan: 'the dog-headed, barking Baboon, who is Quite the Wisest Animal in All South Africa'. The Baviaan is Kipling's invention: 'I have drawn him from a statue that I made up out of my own head.'[7] The ingenuity and detail of the Baviaan figure are carried over into the many different kinds of script that Kipling uses to decorate the image. In their appearance the scripts reflect the look (only) of writing found in Coptic, Egyptian, cuneiform, Persian, Babylonic, Bengali, Burmese and Hebrew (the shapes that Kipling invented spell out the words 'Baviaan' and 'Wise Baviaan'). The inscriptions are picture puzzles for a small child, and they show the pleasure taken in detailed work for its own sake which was deeply ingrained in both Kiplings, Lockwood and Rudyard. This story, probably already in Kipling's mind in 1897, was written early in 1900, during the South African War, in The Woolsack, the house generously made available by Cecil Rhodes* so that the Kipling family could escape the British winters. (The story of Kipling's friendship with Cecil Rhodes is taken further in chapter 5.) The setting of the Leopard story is therefore

---

* Kipling first saw Cecil Rhodes on a brief visit to Cape Town in 1891 and later got to know him in London. Kipling's trip to South Africa in 1898 was specifically in order to stay with Rhodes and support his vision for Africa. Kipling also knew the then High Commissioner, Sir Alfred Milner. His perception of South Africa was determined by the work of these men and by the writings of another friend, Sir Henry Rider Haggard, famous for his African-based historical fantasies *King Solomon's Mines* (1886), *She* (1887) and *Nada the Lily* (1892), the latter of which Kipling said inspired the family of talking wolves in his Mowgli stories. *She*, which Haggard had completed in six weeks, was a sensational bestseller. The friendship between the two writers, recorded in their correspondence, was competitive as well as close.[8]

appropriately South African, with its references to a sun-baked landscape, the ''sclusively bare, hot, shiny High Veldt, where there was sand and sandy-coloured rock'.

The strings of adjectives in the Leopard story draw the child in as a collaborator. The Leopard and the Ethiopian, hunting for food, 'saw a great, high, tall forest full of tree trunks all 'sclusively speckled and sprottled and spottled, dotted and splashed and slashed and hatched and cross-hatched with shadows. (Say that quickly aloud and you will see how *very* shadowy the forest must have been.)'9 The reiteration of ''sclusively' is itself part of the game, the repetitions persisting, until after the fourteenth use of ''sclusively' the child audience would have been helplessly hooked. The ingenious similes keep up the story's carnival spirit: 'you show up in this dark place like a bar of soap in a coal-scuttle', 'you show up in this dark place like a mustard-plaster on a sack of coals', 'you insist on looking like a sunflower against a tarred fence'.10 The Baviaan advises the Leopard and the Ethiopian that they are unsuccessful hunters because they are too visible against the jungle's foliage, while the Giraffe and the Zebra and other beasts of the jungle acquired camouflage covering (mottled patches, stripes, etc.) by spending all their lives under the shadows of the trees in the jungle.

The Leopard and the Ethiopian are hungry, and the story is not about race, or politics, or power, but simply about improving their chances of hunting effectively for food. The freedom from political pressure is calculated and deliberate. The difference between child and adult is not excluded from the tale, though. The Leopard uses a child's discourse, and is to be imagined as the same age as the story's first audience, but his friend and hunting companion, the Ethiopian, is a 'grown-up'.

Said Leopard to Baviaan (and it was a very hot day), 'Where has all the game gone?' [...]

Said the Ethiopian to Baviaan, 'Can you tell me the present habitat of the aboriginal Fauna?' (That meant just the same thing, but the Ethiopian always used long words. He was a grown-up.)

The Baviaan's replies to the two friends turn on rather weak puns (pleasing enough though for a small child):

> Then said Baviaan, 'The game has gone into other spots; and my advice to you, Leopard, is to go into other spots as soon as you can.' And the Ethiopian said, 'That is all very fine, but I wish to know whither the aboriginal Fauna has migrated.'
>
> Then said Baviaan, 'The aboriginal Fauna has joined the aboriginal Flora because it was high time for a change; and my advice to you, Ethiopian, is to change as soon as you can.'[11]

The two friends go into the forest to hunt. The Ethiopian remarks that giraffes 'ought to show up in this dark place like ripe bananas in a smoke-house', but nothing is visible. Accordingly they wait until dark and then each catches a creature which smells like familiar food. 'Leopard heard something breathing sniffily in the starlight that fell all stripy through the branches, and he jumped at the noise, and it smelt like Zebra, and it felt like Zebra, and when he knocked it down it kicked like Zebra', but he is unable to see it: it is a 'person without any form'. The Ethiopian has the same experience with a thing that 'smells like Giraffe, and it kicks like Giraffe, but it hasn't any form'. 'They sat down on them hard till bright morning-time, and then Leopard said, "What have you at your end of the table, Brother?"' The Ethiopian replies that what he has caught 'ought to be 'sclusively a rich fulvous orange-tawny from head to heel, and it ought to be Giraffe; but it is covered all over with chestnut blotches. What have you at *your* end of the table, Brother?' The Leopard has what ought to be a 'delicate grey-ish fawn' Zebra, but it 'is covered all over with black and purple stripes'. The two friends ask the Giraffe and the Zebra why it is that they were invisible ('how is it done?'). Zebra responds with a Brer Rabbit strategy: 'Let us up [...] and we will show you.' The hunters fall into the trap; the Zebra and the Giraffe say, 'This is the way it's done. One-two-three! And where's your breakfast?' and they move into positions where they merge with 'stripy shadows and blotched shadows in the forest'.[12]

Although the Ethiopian is a 'grown-up' and the Leopard is not, when engaged on the urgent task of hunting for food which they cannot see they address each other as 'Brother', allies and equals united by a common purpose. One may reflect here that Kipling's beloved Freemasons spoke to each other as brothers and equals in the Masonic Lodge, although outside it they could be military senior officers who were forbidden to consort with men of lower ranks. They recall the Baviaan's second piece of advice, 'to change as soon as you can': the Ethiopian blacks himself all over and has enough black left on his fingers to imprint the Leopard with his spots.

This compares with the device in 'How Fear Came', from *The Second Jungle Book*, in which Kipling explored a version of the same idea. In this story Hathi the Elephant recounts what is presented as an ancient creation myth. In this myth, Tha, the 'First of the Elephants', creates the Jungle as a peaceful paradise in which fear is unknown. The First of the Tigers destroys this innocence, and introduces fear into the Jungle, by killing a buck. Tha 'gave an order to the trees that hang low, and to the trailing creepers of the Jungle, that they should mark the killer of the buck so that he should know him again'.[13] The difference between this and the story of 'How the Leopard got his Spots' is, of course, that in 'How Fear Came' identification rather than camouflage is the objective.

The image shows 'the Leopard and the Ethiopian after they had taken Wise Baviaan's advice'. The Leopard is now spotted and dappled, to the left of the image, and the Ethiopian, completely black, sits on the right. In the middle distance, with its head reaching for leaves to the right of the image, stands the Giraffe, now successfully disguised by his mottled patterned skin. In his account of the way the Leopard and the Ethiopian camouflage themselves Kipling sidesteps the question of racial discrimination. He had become fond of these two characters and the combination of affection and literary tact was guiding him here. He was

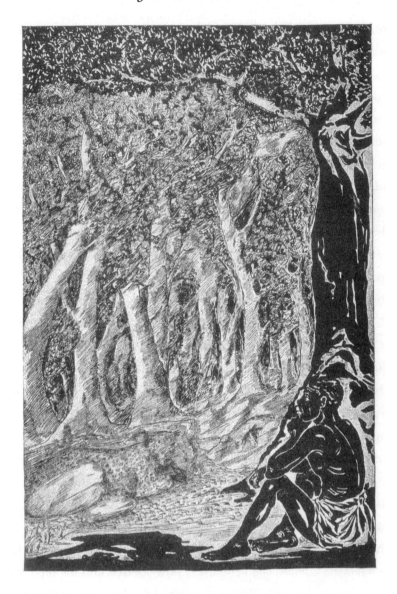

also trusting his personal 'Daemon', the providence that he felt guided the pen when he was at his best.[14]

The Ethiopian goes to the heart of the problem: ' "The long and the little of it is that we don't match our backgrounds. I'm going to take Baviaan's advice. He told me I ought to change; and as I've nothing to change except my skin I'm going to change that." "What to?" said the

Leopard, tremendously excited' ('excited' because, unlike the Ethiopian, he is not 'grown-up'). 'To a nice working blackish-brownish colour, with a little purple in it, and touches of slaty-blue. It will be the very thing for hiding in hollows and behind trees.'[15] The Leopard ('more excited than ever; he had never seen a man change his skin before') asks about his own disguise. The Ethiopian responds with further wordplay:

> 'You take Baviaan's advice too. He told you to go into spots.' 'So I did,' said the Leopard. 'I went into other spots as soon as I could. I went into this spot with you, and a lot of good it has done me.' 'Oh,' said the Ethiopian, 'Baviaan didn't mean spots in South Africa. He meant spots on your skin.'[16]

The procedure is described, with some tenderness, as one of the friends modifies the body of the other:

> Then the Ethiopian put his five fingers close together (there was plenty of black left on his new skin still) and pressed them all over the Leopard, and wherever the five fingers touched they left five little black marks, all close together. You can see them on any Leopard's skin you like, Best Beloved. Sometimes the fingers slipped and the marks got a little blurred; but if you look closely at any Leopard now you will see that there are always five spots – off five fat black finger-tips.

The Leopard asks why the Ethiopian did not choose to make himself equally spotty, and his reply is simple and direct, though its choice of words may give a jolt to a reader in the twenty-first century:

> 'Oh, plain black's best for a nigger,' said the Ethiopian. 'Now come along and we'll see if we can't get even with Mr One-Two-Three-Where's-your-Breakfast!' So they went away and lived happily ever afterward, Best Beloved. That is all.[17]

The caption to the second image in the story raises a related scruple where it gives the names of the Leopard and the Ethiopian: 'The Ethiopian was really a negro, and so his name was Sambo. The Leopard was called Spots.' Kipling's choice of words here again needs to be understood clearly within its context. 'Sambo' reflects the title of a popular children's story of the day, *Little Black Sambo*, published by the Scottish writer Helen Bannerman in 1899. Nothing derogatory was intended by the name, it was an affectionate and playful familiar nursery term of the period. Four tigers take possession of Sambo's clothes, they then compete with each other over which looks most splendid and they pursue each other round a tree until they are melted down into *ghi* (melted butter). Black Sambo's mother uses the *ghi* to make pancakes (Sambo eats 169 pancakes, a heroic number and a mark of virtue triumphant, we may take it). 'They went away and lived happily ever afterward' – this phrasing securely seals the frame of the story, and places it among fairy-tales.

After leaving Vermont and returning to England in 1896 the Kiplings had settled at first by the sea, at St Marychurch in Devon. Carrie did not get on with Alice Kipling and was happy to live at a safe distance from her parents-in-law at Tisbury, but Devon did not suit Kipling – it was too far from London where his friends and his audience were centred – and within a few months the Kiplings were moving house again, first to Torquay and from there to Rottingdean, where Kipling's beloved Uncle Ned (Burne-Jones) owned a house.

The year 1899 marked their final break with America. Rottingdean and then his parents' home at Tisbury and thereafter (from 1902) his own home at Bateman's, Burwash, in Sussex, became the bases for Kipling's operations. He chose not to visit India again, declining an invitation to Delhi for the Coronation Durbar in 1902. It is likely that he was shrinking from the memories of lost love. The India of his childhood had been idyllic, and his emotional attachment to it had been so strong that the new, changing India of the Edwardian period did not appeal to him.

How the Leopard got his Spots

The Kiplings were also establishing what would become the annual rhythm of their escapes to South Africa from the English winter. Andrew Lycett claims that in Africa Kipling's ''satiable curtiosity' deserted him. He liked its landscapes and the beauty of its sea-coasts 'but otherwise gave no indication of seeing the continent as anything except a part in a giant jigsaw puzzle that needed assembling for the furtherance of Empire'.[18] The exception to this is Kipling's Ethiopian in the Leopard story, but beyond that it is broadly true. Kipling chose not to engage with the black Africans among whom he spent his winters in Cape Town. In a letter from December 1900 he makes a brief reference to an African-American tragedy which exposes an offhand, callous prejudice, and has the dismaying effect of binding together Kipling the doting father and Kipling the unthinking racist. Kipling was due to take his family to South Africa again. These winter trips were increasingly for Carrie's benefit (Kipling wrote that the 'pestilent British weather' had made her ill and 'sunshine and clean air' would pull her round again). Kipling had been teaching Elsie how to play Beggar-my-neighbour. 'She solemnly reported to her nurse that "she had learnt a new game with Daddy called Govern-my-Negro!!!" They ought to introduce it into the Southern States – and Colorado.'[19] Why Colorado? Kipling had been reading a US report about 'Preston Porter, a sixteen-year-old negro, [who] was burned at the stake in Limon, Colorado, on 16 November [1900]; the fire was lit by the father of the girl that Porter had murdered.'[20] Kipling's jokiness regarding this grisly event exhibits an aspect of him that one would prefer not to have to acknowledge.

We can single out 'How the Leopard got his Spots' as an account of an African who does not experience this kind of horrible prejudice. The Ethiopian and his friend the Leopard hunt together. The two friends in their pastoral African landscape echo other fictional friendships such as those of Huckleberry Finn and Tom Sawyer, or Pooh and Piglet in their Sussex landscape of Ashdown Forest a generation later. The Leopard story is a dance and a configuration of patterns where skin colour becomes a subject for reflection on adaptation and habitat. The dominant features of the tale are its playfulness and its fascination with technique and verbal invention.

A younger Kipling, working as a journalist in Lahore, had written a long journal-letter to his cousin Margaret Burne-Jones (28 November 1885–11 January 1886) in which he considered the whole question of racial tensions in the empire. Margaret had asked about relations between the English imperial rulers and the 'natives' in India. Kipling replied:

> When you write 'native' who do you mean? The Mahommedan who hates the Hindu; the Hindu who hates the Mahommedan; the Sikh who loathes both; or the semi-anglicized product of our Indian colleges who is hated and despised by Sikh, Hindu and Mahommedan. Do you mean the Punjabi who will have nothing do to with the Bengali; the Mahrattha to whom the Punjabi's tongue is as incomprehensible as Russian to me; the Parsee who controls the whole trade of Bombay and ranges himself on all questions as an Englishman; the Sindee who is an outsider; the Bhil or the Gond who is an aborigine; the Rajput who despises everything on God's earth but himself; the Delhi traders who control trade to the value of millions; the Afghan who is only kept from looting these same merchants by dread of English interference. Which one of all the thousand conflicting tongues, races, nationalities and peoples between the Khaibar Pass and Ceylon do you mean?[21]

Here Kipling was both claiming an insider's knowledge of a complex situation and defending the British control of India from the more liberal attitudes of the Burne-Jones family. At the same time he was distancing himself from the 'wholly wrong attitude of mind' of the typical unthinking Englishman who is 'prone to despise' the Indian people, and he contrasts this with his own sympathetic intimacy with the street life of Lahore. (Writing fast, and probably late at night, he uses what he rightly calls the 'misleading term "native"' as shorthand for the Indian people.) Their life 'runs wholly untouched and unaffected' by the British. Lahore is a city of 'night houses, night strolls with natives; evenings spent in their company in their own homes (in the men's quarter of course) and the long yarns that my native friends spin me.'[22] His father's work in Lahore has given him privileged access. 'A man who has the confidence of the natives can do *anything* ... The Mahommedans in the city know my Pater and almost worship him in many ways, for the things he's done.'[23]

5

THE ELEPHANT'S CHILD

In the High and Far-Off Times the Elephant, O Best Beloved, had no trunk.* He had only a blackish, bulgy nose, as big as a boot, that he could wriggle about from side to side; but he couldn't pick up things with it. But there was one Elephant – a new Elephant – an Elephant's Child – who was full of 'satiable curtiosity, and that means he asked ever so many questions. *And* he lived in Africa, and he filled all Africa with his 'satiable curtiosities. He asked his tall aunt, the Ostrich, why her tail-feathers grew just so, and his tall aunt the Ostrich spanked him with her hard, hard claw. He asked his tall uncle, the Giraffe, what made his skin spotty, and his tall uncle, the Giraffe, spanked him with his hard, hard hoof. And still he was full of 'satiable curtiosity! He asked his broad aunt, the Hippopotamus, why her eyes were red, and his broad aunt, the Hippopotamus, spanked him with her broad, broad hoof; and he asked his hairy uncle, the Baboon, why melons tasted just so, and his hairy uncle, the Baboon, spanked him with his hairy, hairy paw. And still he was full of 'satiable curtiosity! He asked questions about everything that he saw, or heard, or felt, or smelt, or touched, and all his uncles and his aunts spanked him. And still he was full of 'satiable curtiosity!

One fine morning in the middle of the Precession of the Equinoxes this 'satiable Elephant's Child asked a new fine question that he had

---

* Folio 38 of the *Just so* manuscript gives the original elephant as not only trunkless but also very small. 'The elephant, oh best beloved, was no more than a tapir – a twinkling tapir – and that was how he always behaved.'[1]

never asked before. He asked 'What does the Crocodile have for dinner?'
Then everybody said, 'Hush!' in a loud and dretful tone, and they spanked
him immediately and directly, without stopping, for a long time.[2]

The 'Precession of the Equinoxes' would have prompted Kipling's child
audience to ask what this phrase meant and why it is in the tale. The
tale itself offers no answer. Kipling is not going over the heads of his
child audience to wink in mutual knowingness at an adult third party.
Rather, he is extending the child's own 'satiable curtiosity. Small children
like the challenge of unfamiliar words. 'Precession' was part of a reading
of the universe by classical Greek astronomers who proposed that the
constellations moved round the earth in a slow cycle lasting roughly
26,000 years (often referred to as 'the Platonic Year'). If the Elephant's
Child's adventure takes place in the middle of this time span, this lends an
elegant symmetry to Kipling's alternative creation myth. The Child
acquires his trunk at precisely the midpoint of the world's prehistory.

The text deploys a wordplay passage which is not quite nonsensical:
'That very next morning, when there was nothing left of the Equinoxes,
because the Precession had preceded according to precedent', the Child
sets out. His preparation for the trip involves an amassing of detail:

> This 'satiable Elephant's Child took a hundred pounds of bananas (the
> little short red kind), and a hundred pounds of sugar-cane (the long
> purple kind), and seventeen melons (the greeny-crackly kind), and
> said to all his dear families, 'Good-bye. I am going to the great grey-
> green, greasy Limpopo River, all set about with fever-trees, to find out
> what the Crocodile has for dinner.' And they all spanked him once
> more for luck, though he asked them most politely to stop.[3]

The Elephant's Child is persistent and obstinate. These were
characteristics of Kipling himself and are perhaps the necessary
characteristics of any writer, given that writing for the marketplace

requires hard work and sturdy self-belief. The growth, adaptability and resilience of the Elephant's Child show parallels with Kipling's own early life, and in this respect 'The Elephant's Child' is the most personal of all the *Just so Stories*. The Elephant's Child can be seen as John Lockwood Kipling's child.

The Child 'had never seen a Crocodile, and did not know what one was like. It was all his 'satiable curtiosity'. The 'curtiosity' leads him to the great grey-green Limpopo River where he encounters a Bi-Coloured-Python-Rock-Snake curled round a rock. The Elephant's Child asks his inevitable question (what does the Crocodile have for dinner?) with the predictable consequence: 'Then the Bi-Coloured-Python-Rock-Snake uncoiled himself very quickly from the rock, and spanked the Elephant's Child with his scalesome, flailsome tail.'[4] The Child, now 'a little warm' after the beating 'but not at all astonished', makes his way to the bank of the Limpopo and there encounters the Crocodile himself. The Elephant's Child greets the Crocodile with his memorable malapropism: 'do you happen to have seen a Crocodile in these promiscuous parts?'

The Elephant's Child takes an extreme risk: ' "Will you please tell me what you have for dinner?" "Come hither, Little One," said the Crocodile, "and I'll whisper." ' There should be authentic frisson here. When the story is read aloud the reader needs to dig deep for the husky register of a falsely reassuring grandfather who could also be a child abuser.

> Then the Elephant's Child put his head down close to the Crocodile's musky, tusky mouth, and the Crocodile caught him by his little nose, which up to that very week, day, hour, and minute, had been no bigger than a boot, though much more useful.
>
> 'I think,' said the Crocodile – and he said it between his teeth like this – 'I think today I will begin with Elephant's Child!'[5]

The Rock-Snake, in pedantic parody of a learned adult, intervenes at this point with elaborately phrased advice:

The Elephant's Child

'My young friend, if you do not now, immediately and instantly, pull as hard as ever you can, it is my opinion that your acquaintance in the large-pattern leather ulster' (and by this he meant the Crocodile) 'will jerk you into yonder limpid stream before you can say Jack Robinson.' This is the way Bi-Coloured-Python-Rock-Snakes always talk. Then the Elephant's Child sat back on his little haunches, and pulled, and pulled, and pulled, and his nose began to stretch. And the Crocodile floundered into the water, making it all creamy with great sweeps of his tail, and *he* pulled, and pulled, and pulled.

And the Elephant's Child's nose kept on stretching; and the Elephant's Child spread all his little four legs and pulled, and pulled,

and pulled, and his nose kept on stretching; and the Crocodile threshed his tail like an oar, and *he* pulled, and pulled, and pulled, and at each pull the Elephant's Child's nose grew longer and longer – and it hurt him hijjus![6]

The Bi-Coloured-Python-Rock-Snake 'knotted himself in a double-clove-hitch round the Elephant's Child's hind-legs' and delivers further finely honed counsel:

'Rash and inexperienced traveller, we will now seriously devote ourselves to a little high tension, because if we do not, it is my impression that yonder self-propelling man-of-war with the armour-plated upper deck' (and by this, O Best Beloved, he meant the Crocodile) 'will permanently vitiate your future career.'

That is the way all Bi-Coloured-Python-Rock-Snakes always talk.[7]

In the ensuing tug of war the Elephant's Child and the Bi-Coloured-Python-Rock-Snake pull hardest and 'at last the Crocodile let go of the Elephant's Child's nose with a plop that you could hear all up and down the Limpopo'. The Child 'was kind to his poor pulled nose, and wrapped it all up in cool banana leaves, and hung it in the great grey-green, greasy Limpopo to cool'. The Rock-Snake points out that 'Some people do not know what is good for them', and the narrator spells out the Elephant Child's good fortune:

The Elephant's Child sat there for three days waiting for his nose to shrink. But it never grew any shorter, and, besides, it made him squint. For, O Best Beloved, you will see and understand that the Crocodile had pulled it out into a really truly trunk same as all Elephants have today.[8]

The Child discovers the value and versatility of his new trunk: 'When he wanted fruit to eat he pulled fruit down from a tree, instead of waiting for it to fall as he used to do.' The commentary continues:

When he wanted grass he plucked grass up from the ground, instead of going on his knees as he used to do. When the flies bit him he broke off the branch of a tree and used it as a fly-whisk; and he made himself a new, cool, slushy-squshy mud-cap whenever the sun was hot. When he felt lonely walking through Africa he sang to himself down his trunk, and the noise was louder than several brass bands.[9]

When the Elephant's Child completes his journey the story shifts from its primary interest in his changing body and becomes a tale of revenge. The Child returns to 'all his dear families'.

They were very glad to see him, and immediately said, 'Come here and be spanked for your 'satiable curtiosity.' 'Pooh!' said the Elephant's Child. 'I don't think you peoples know anything about spanking; but *I* do, and I'll show you.' Then he uncurled his trunk and knocked two of his dear brothers head over heels.[10]

An orgy of retribution follows: 'that bad Elephant's Child spanked all his dear families for a long time, till they were very warm and greatly astonished'. The whole species then follows his example so that its evolutionary transformation is achieved overnight: 'his dear families went off one by one in a hurry to the banks of the great grey-green, greasy Limpopo River, all set about with fever-trees, to borrow new noses from the Crocodile. When they came back nobody spanked anybody anymore.'[11]

The Elephant having his nose pulled by the Crocodile is the best known of all Kipling's images for the *Just so Stories*. As in the image of the Djinn giving the Camel his Hump, there is a second image, a predella. Like the predella to the Camel image this one also has Noah's Ark (floating, inside a triangular frame). This Ark (which we recognise as the rebus for Kipling's initials, RK) has toy African animals processing into it. Kipling pretends not to know what all the animals are: 'There are two lions, two ostriches, two oxen, two camels, two sheep, and two other things that look like rats, but I think they are rock-rabbits. They don't mean anything. I put them in because I thought they looked pretty. They would look very fine if I were allowed to paint them.' The caption to the image of the Elephant pulling bananas off a banana-tree collaborates with the reader in the same way: 'I don't think it is a very nice picture; but I couldn't make it any better, because elephants and bananas are hard to draw.' He adds, teasingly: 'I think it would look better if you painted the banana-tree green and the Elephant's Child red.'[12]

The images of the Elephant himself are modelled on the Indian elephant, but the story's setting, South Africa, was a country that Kipling came to love for its climate and its landscapes. He had recently travelled (in March 1898) the Child's route (through what is now Botswana): 'He went from Graham's Town to Kimberley, and from Kimberley to Khama's Country, and from Khama's Country he went east by north, eating melons all the time, till at last he came to the banks of the great grey-green, greasy Limpopo River, all set about with fever-trees, precisely as Kolokolo Bird had said.'[13] (The melons are important: the Elephant's Child travels 'throwing the rind about' because he does not yet have a fully developed trunk.)

By the time Kipling was writing 'The Elephant's Child' he had established a close relationship with Cecil Rhodes, and was taking annual winter holidays in South Africa with Carrie and the children as Rhodes' guest. Kipling idolised this rich, silent, powerful man. Rhodes' personality was in some respects surprisingly simple. Kipling said that Rhodes had a habit of 'jerking out sudden questions as disconcerting as those of a child – or the Roman Emperor he so much resembled. He said to me apropos of nothing in particular: "What's your dream?" I answered that he was part of it.'[14] Kipling became one of Rhodes' most valued courtiers. 'My use to him was as a purveyor of words; for he was largely inarticulate. After the idea had been presented – and one had to know his code for it – he would say: "what am I trying to express? Say it, *say* it." So I would say it, and if the phrase suited not, he would work it over, chin a little down, till it satisfied him.'[15]

Kipling's hero-worship of Rhodes aligned itself with his growing authoritarianism, and his sense of the moral superiority of the British as against the Dutch. If read quickly and superficially, 'Recessional', written in the year of Queen Victoria's Diamond Jubilee, 1897, can be seen as the work of an unreconstructed late Victorian racist. The poem is actually from the quite different Kipling who had two sides to his head and could immerse himself fully in Indian culture, as in *Kim*. Also, like the *Just so Stories*, it reflects Kipling's deep knowledge of the Bible. In the 1890s the British Empire was seen as Christian, benevolent, enlightening to the younger nations and so forth, but it was also acknowledged by some that that confidence might have been misplaced. The occasion of Queen Victoria's Jubilee caused Kipling to write a hymn which challenged the prevailing mood. The Diamond Jubilee of 1897 was the occasion of great rejoicing throughout the British Empire, and the ceremonies were a demonstration of unprecedented imperial togetherness. Beneath its celebrations, however, there were currents of uneasiness. 'Recessional' sounded a note of caution. It reminded the people, wild with excitement and patriotism, that they should not forget God – 'Lest we forget – lest we forget!' – and that 'for frantic boast and foolish word' the nation should be crying for mercy: 'Thy mercy on Thy People, Lord!' Kipling's hymn, with its remembrance of what happened to Nineveh and Tyre, and its cry to the 'Lord God of Hosts', was a striking condemnation of pride and complacency.

God of our fathers, known of old,
Lord of our far-flung battle-line,
Beneath whose awful Hand we hold
Dominion over palm and pine –
Lord God of Hosts, be with us yet,
Lest we forget – lest we forget!

Psalm 51 is written in a spirit of extreme humility, and is much quoted in prayers and church anthems of contrition: 'Wash me thoroughly from mine iniquity', for example, 'hide thy face from my sins, and blot out all mine iniquities', and especially, 'the sacrifices of God are a broken spirit: a broken and a contrite heart, O God, thou wilt not despise'. This spirit informs Kipling's poem, especially its second stanza:

> The tumult and the shouting dies;
> The Captains and the Kings depart:
> Still stands Thine ancient sacrifice,
> An humble and a contrite heart.
> Lord God of Hosts, be with us yet,
> Lest we forget – lest we forget![16]

This poem's famous refrain, 'Lest we forget', is adapted from Deuteronomy 6:12: 'Then beware lest thou forget the Lord, which brought thee forth out of the land of Egypt, from the house of bondage.' In other words, do not become arrogant, keep the humility of those who know that there is a higher power. There is an inherent contradiction here between tenor and vehicle. The poem's burden is 'be humble' and 'avoid racial arrogance', but at the same time its music, and much of its vocabulary, are triumphalist, especially in the address to the 'God of our fathers, known of old', who has granted 'dominion over palm and pine' to the British. As Harry Ricketts puts it, the poem 'was simply not humble.'[17]

When he was writing his autobiography in 1935, Kipling recalled the public mood of 1897. The English of that date, the wealthiest and most powerful people in the world, had become complacent and insular ('the inhabitants of that country never looked further than their annual seaside resorts'), while Kipling, with his international perspective, feared threats to Britain's power. He expressed this in a quotation from II Samuel 5:24: 'a sound of a going in the tops of the mulberry trees'. The 'sound of a going', the premonition of a storm, was at odds with the national mood. 'Into the middle of it all came the Great Queen's Diamond Jubilee, and a certain optimism that scared me.' Hence 'Recessional', written to avert disaster (a *nuzzur-wattu* or averter of the Evil Eye, as Kipling calls it).[18]

The poem's warning is like that given in I Chronicles 29:10–18, where David speaks in both celebration and warning of the temple which Solomon is to complete: 'We are strangers before thee, and sojourners, as were all our fathers: our days on the earth are as a shadow, and there is none abiding [...] O Lord God of Abraham, Isaac, and of Israel, our fathers, keep this forever in the imagination of the thoughts and hearts of thy people.' Romans 2:14 underlies the most controversial lines of the poem:

> If, drunk with sight of power, we loose
> Wild tongues that have not Thee in awe,
> Such boastings as the Gentiles use,
> Or lesser breeds without the Law –
> Lord God of Hosts, be with us yet,
> Lest we forget – lest we forget![19]

It is just about possible to defend the notorious line about 'lesser breeds' by asserting that the phrase refers not to race but to culture, and does not refer to the difference between black and white skin (the contest was between European powers seeking to control Africa, a struggle in which Germans and the Dutch South Africans are seen as living by codes different from those of the British). Still, there is a real problem, neatly defined by Elliot L. Gilbert: 'the poem repeatedly implies values which directly contradict those it explicitly endorses'. The line about dominion over palm and pine points to 'some sort of supernal ratification of Britain's imperial destiny'. The phrase 'lesser breeds' urges England 'to be contrite principally on the grounds that the chosen of God ought to be more scrupulous than anyone else'.

> What is dismaying about the line [with its phrase 'lesser breeds'] is its inherent act of 'presuming to judge' in the context of a poem whose

ostensible subject is the arrogance of such judgements. Thus, the failure of 'Recessional' is aesthetic not political, and thus 'lesser breeds without the Law' fails as a line of poetry much more importantly than it does as a political utterance.[20]

Kipling committed himself fully to Rhodes' project in South Africa, which meant, inevitably, that when war broke out between the British, supported by Rhodes, and the two independent Dutch colonies, the Orange Free State and the Transvaal, Kipling put his talents wholeheartedly at the disposal of the British assailants. His poem 'The Old Issue', published in *The Times* on 29 September 1899, reads today like a crazily unbalanced piece of special pleading. The conflict with the Dutch settlers was a 'war for liberty', with the Dutch cast as the tyrants.[21] In the same week that this poem was published Kipling was writing 'The Elephant's Child' in which the same landscape becomes an arena in which the Child engages in his playful power-struggle with his 'dear families'. Is there some echo of English resistance to the Dutch in the Child's determination to show his 'dear families' that they know nothing about spanking?

'Of Elephants', chapter IX of Lockwood Kipling's *Beast and Man in India*, treats the animal with mystical regard. 'The Elephant', he wrote, 'has always been one of the wonders of the world, amazing in his aspect and full of delightful and surprising qualities. Next after the cow [which was sacred] he seems to be of all the beasts the Hindu favourite.' Muslims, by contrast – the 'Muhammad and Nawab' – prefer the horse.[22] Elephant sculptures are rated by Lockwood as the most distinguished products of Hindu art, displaying at all times what he calls (with Ruskinian fervour) a 'strong feeling for nature'. This is a feature of elephant images 'in most old temples, but especially in the sculptured gates [. . .] in Central India, where all kinds of animals are shown, but the elephant alone is carved with complete knowledge, and unvarying truth of action'. British writers, John Lockwood suggests, are not successful with elephants:

Dickens said long ago that the elephant employs the worst tailor in all the world. But these wrinkled columns suggest feminine grace to the Oriental poet, and 'elephant-gaited' is the supreme and also the invariable expression for the voluptuous movements of women: 'A voice as sweet as that of the Koil, and a gait as voluptuous as that of the elephant: An eye like an antelope's, a waist like the lion's, and a gait like the elephant's,' are specimens of an endless series of descriptions of female beauty.[23]

Two of his most detailed images in *Beast and Man* show two stages in an elephant's day. In the first the elephant is being cared for in its compound, while the second shows the same animal, now ceremonially dressed, waiting to take part in a Raja's procession. Lockwood Kipling noted that elephants bring good luck in most Indian traditions. Ganésa, Ganesh or Ganpati, the elephant god, part human and part elephant, is 'the wise and humorous god who is invoked at the beginning of all enterprises, whose auspicious image is placed over most Hindu doorways'. Ganesh is the product of mistaken identity. Parvati, wife of the god Shiva, diverted herself in her husband's absence by making a live baby out of clay. Shiva, arriving unexpectedly, thought the baby was evidence of adultery on Parvati's part and cut off its head. When he learnt of his mistake he immediately put it right by cutting off the head of a passing elephant and putting it on the baby.[24] Ganesh is a god of advancement and good fortune. His sign is a swastika, which is also a symbol in Freemasonry. Kipling adopted this decorative feature for the front matter of many of his books until the 1930s.

It seems that the germ of 'The Elephant's Child' came from a small American child, Nelson Doubleday, the son of Kipling's American publisher, F.N. Doubleday. Nelson recalled that after being given 'How the Whale got his Throat' to read as a boy he wrote to Kipling suggesting further subjects: 'how the leopard got his spots, how the elephant got his trunk, about the crocodile

and so on'. Several literary traditions feed into 'The Elephant's Child': talking animal stories, revenge stories, and stories of personal growth.

A number of Kipling's short stories featured revenge, particularly those in his collection of 1899, *Stalky & Co.* This book had disappointed many of its readers ('only the spoilt child of an utterly brutalised public could possibly have written *Stalky & Co.*', one reviewer wrote),[25] and many of the schoolboy revenges in it are brash and distasteful. In 'The Elephant's Child', by contrast, the Child's spankings of his 'dear families' are sanitised and firmly contained within the story's pattern (all the elephants learn from the experience to go and get themselves trunks from the Crocodile; another Lamarckian moment in which adaptation is achieved by an act of will).

'The Elephant's Child' is about a growing youngster who becomes fully himself. This is the theme of a long tradition in mainstream English fiction, including such famous examples as Fielding's *Tom Jones* (1749) and Dickens' *David Copperfield*. Both Tom and David are ill-treated as children and both survive those experiences to become competent and balanced adults. Kipling, by contrast, did not reach that plateau of adulthood. His disturbed childhood remained with him all his life.*

As a coming-of-age narrative, 'The Elephant's Child' can be compared with the stories of Mowgli in the two *Jungle Books*. 'Mowgli's Brothers', the story which tells of Mowgli's arrival in the wolf's cave and his adoption by the wolf family, was not the first of the Mowgli stories to be published. That was 'In the Rukh' (a 'Rukh' is a forest), which had been included in Kipling's *Many Inventions* (1893). This Mowgli is a somewhat shallow theatrical invention (a bit like the Pan figures in stories of the period by E.M. Forster, Arthur Machen and Kenneth Grahame). He is 'naked except for the loin-cloth, but crowned with a wreath of the tasselled blossoms of the white convolvulus creeper' and his face 'as he lifted it into the sunshine might have been that of an angel strayed among the woods'.[30] He offers to share his knowledge of the forest with a character called Gisborne, who is a British forestry officer.[31] Happily, Kipling adopted a wholly different manner for the figure of Mowgli in the two *Jungle Books*, where Mowgli and his animal companions speak a kind of biblical English to each other.

---

* For Harry Ricketts the abusive experience at Southsea fed directly into Kipling's Mowgli stories. There is a 'pattern of abandonment' whereby Mowgli becomes in effect 'a super-orphan'.[26] In this reading Shere Khan, the malevolent tiger who wants to eat Mowgli, stood for Mrs Holloway, and his sidekick, Tabaqui the jackal, for her son.[27] To compensate, Mowgli has a 'queue of would-be foster-parents, falling over each other to look after him: Father and Mother Wolf, Akela the Lone Wolf, Baloo the Bear, Bagheera the Black Panther and Kaa the Python'.[28] *The Jungle Book* could not have been conceived without the Southsea 'orphanhood', but it was living in America that allowed Kipling imaginatively to revisit those years and convert loss into gain.[29]

Taken as a group, the narratives give Mowgli's story from his infancy to his adolescence. The child who has dropped out of human society to be cherished and educated by talking animals is offered to us as a member of an ideal community. Mowgli learns a moral and legal code which makes sense within the strict terms of Kipling's invention. Unlike the beatings inflicted by Mrs Holloway, the punishments of Mowgli by the bear and the panther, Baloo and Bagheera, are experienced by the reader as irreproachable because they ensure Mowgli's survival. The writing draws us into his imagined world to a point where the impossible (talking animals creating their own ordered society) feels inevitable. Stories of wolves nurturing human children were among the books in Lockwood Kipling's library, and he wrote that 'India is probably the cradle of wolf-child stories, which are here universally believed and supported by a cloud of testimony.'[32]

'Mowgli's Brothers' (1894) operates well in terms of both myth and natural justice, and is written with such confidence that we do not question its assumptions. Mowgli as a baby wanders into the wolves' lair, claims a warm space by Mother Wolf, and is hunted by the demonic figure of Shere Khan, the tiger who has upset the fundamental moral balance of the jungle by hunting and eating humans. Mowgli's safety with the wolves is assured by his own courage. Mother Wolf's 'How little! How naked, and – how bold!'[33] (as the human baby pushes his way into the cave) enlists her on the side of human against tiger. The story endorses the instinctive savagery with which she defends the child (something Kipling's own mother had failed to do for him when he was 5 years old). 'Father Wolf looked on amazed. He had almost forgotten the days when he won Mother Wolf in fair fight from five other wolves, when she ran in the Pack and was not called The Demon for compliments sake.'[34]

In *The Second Jungle Book*, though, the story called 'Letting in the Jungle' upsets the previous stories' confident sense of natural justice by admitting a destabilising streak of European prejudice. Terrified by the behaviour of Mowgli's wolf family, all the inhabitants of an

Indian village turn on a couple who have harboured Mowgli in order to protect him:

> The village had got hold of Messua and her husband, who were undoubtedly the father and mother of this Devil-child, and had barricaded them in their own hut, and presently would torture them to make them confess they were witch and wizard, and then they would be burnt to death. [...] But, said the charcoal-burners, what would happen if the English heard of it? The English, they had heard, were a perfectly mad people, who would not let honest farmers kill witches in peace.[35]

The Indian villagers are seen here as morally stunted, childlike in their cruelty, and therefore requiring government by the English. Further, revenge as a moral force is bluntly praised in Mowgli's reflection on what he does to the village when he urges his animal allies to destroy it: 'It was after the letting in of the Jungle that the pleasantest part of Mowgli's life began. He had the good conscience that comes from paying debts.'[36] This state has to pass, because Mowgli is a fostered alien (as the child Kipling had been in Southsea). As he grows into an adolescent his instincts force him to leave the jungle and join a native village. Fable, as used in both the *Just so Stories* and the *Jungle Books*, invites readers to reflect on real experience and on the structures, social and emotional, which support and confer identity. For Kipling himself as boy and man these structures were never secure; his sense of his own identity would remain fluid and protean.

Kim (1901) established Kipling beyond doubt as a major writer. The first stirrings of *Kim* belong to the year in which Kipling was inspired to think about the *Just so Stories*. In a letter from Brattleboro of 15 October 1892 to Mary Mapes Dodge he playfully outlines the central dramatic structure of *Kim* (as though it is a half-remembered anecdote):

> Did you ever hear of [...] the small boy who got a blessing and a ghost-dagger from a Thibetan lama who came down from Thibet in

search of a miraculous river that washed away all sin (the river that gushed out when the Bodhisat's arrow struck the ground) and how these two went hunting for it together – the old priest with his priestly tam o'shanter hat and the young English child?[37]

This letter shows how closely associated in Kipling's mind were the composition of *Kim* and of the *Just so Stories*. With the same anecdotal framing device ('Did you ever hear?'), Noah's Ark (a key symbol in the *Just so Stories*) and the lama with his boy companion are juxtaposed.

Did you ever hear of [. . .] the small boy who made himself a Noah's ark on an Indian tank and filled it with animals and how they wouldn't agree, and how the dove wouldn't fly for the olive branch and how Noah was ingloriously dragged to the bank with all his ark and spanked?[38]

When *Kim* came to be written out in full the child is specifically Irish rather than 'English'; this is an important feature of whole novel's texture and colouring.* Kipling called the novel his 'long leisurely Asiatic yarn in which there are hardly any Englishmen. It has been a labour of great love and I think it is a bit more temperate and wise than much of my stuff.'[40] This book was again a project in which his father was closely involved. For the 1901 Macmillan edition of *Kim* Lockwood Kipling made illustrations which are the products of an interesting experiment: photographic plates of ten low-relief terracotta plaques. The image of the lama, his age and experience indicated by the rough texture of the bas-relief, in company

---

* As Edward Said has said, *Kim* can be related to two historical narrative traditions: by celebrating the friendship of two men in a difficult environment it echoes the 'cultural motif long associated with picaresque tales' in which a male adventurer and his male companion 'are engaged in the pursuit of a special dream – like Jason, Odysseus, or, even more compellingly, Don Quixote with Sancho Panza'. Said adds that the novel is also Chaucerian: 'Kipling has the Middle English poet's eye for wayward detail, the odd character, the slice of life, the amused sense of human foibles and joys.'[39]

with Kim, his young *chela*, is one of the most successful of these images. Kipling wrote in his autobiography that his father was disappointed by the results when he saw the proofs of the book and wanted it 'done again from the beginning', but that they would both now have to wait to recreate *Kim* 'in a better world, and on a scale to amaze the Archangels'.[41]

The talking animal fables in Kipling's *Just so Stories* explore the ways in which creatures find their identities and their true forms (in the Camel,

Leopard, Kangaroo, Armadillo and Elephant stories), and on a much larger scale *Kim* displays the stages by which the boy Kim finds his identity in the course of his shared quest with his lama. The lama is seeking his sacred river and Kim seeks the 'red bull on a green field' spoken of by his drunken Irish father, Kimball O'Hara. The bull is part of the insignia of the Mavericks, the regiment in which Kimball O'Hara had served as a private soldier. The Mavericks pitch camp in a wood where Kim and the lama are taking refuge. Kim recognises that his myth has become reality. The full significance of Kim's birth as a European (Irish) 'sahib' is revealed to him, and he finds it bewildering and unwelcome.[42]

The adolescent Kim suffers much as the adolescent Mowgli does, torn between conflicting identities. Kim's double identity is not resolved by the novel's ending. He is two people. In terms of his new role he is an agent of the British intelligence services in India but in his own emotional understanding of himself he is still the '*chela*' or disciple of his Tibetan lama. The novel's ending finds stasis through the skill with which Kipling gives the closing perspective to the lama. The lama is certain that his quest is concluded and that he has arrived at the Buddhist's destination of full enlightenment. He is given the novel's last reported speech: 'Son of my Soul, I have wrenched my Soul back from the Threshold of Freedom to free thee from all sin.'[43] The whole text closes with the lama's quiet triumph: 'He crossed his hands on his lap and smiled, as a man may who has won Salvation for himself and his beloved.' By placing the lama centre stage so strongly at its close the narrative arrives at a satisfying balance between the mutually exclusive systems which are united in the person of Kim. Also, like the animals in the *Just so* fables, Kim has become fully himself.

Kim's artistic success is in part the product of Kipling's open-mindedness as he wrote the book. Although in the end the political narrative in *Kim* aligns itself with the work of the British intelligence in India, for most of its length it invites the reader to see Kim, the boy, as a free figure who is at one with the country that he loves. For Angus Wilson the boy Kim is 'the Ariel of Kipling's Indian magic kingdom, who goes alike unchecked and unscathed'.[44] The artist in Kipling was following his Daemon; his sympathies in this novel can turn on a sixpence and most of the text displays an open, generous pluralism. *Kim* gives a child growing into a young man, and the story of the Elephant's Child gives a magic version of the similar transformation of the Elephant.

The *Just so Stories* respond to small children's questions about the origins of things, and 'The Elephant's Child' closes with a poem about questions. The 'person small' in this poem is Kipling's second daughter, Elsie, born in Vermont in February 1896.

I keep six honest serving-men
(They taught me all I knew);
Their names are What and Why and When
And How and Where and Who.
I send them over land and sea,
I send them east and west;
But after they have worked for me,
I give them all a rest.

I let them rest from nine till five,
For I am busy then,
As well as breakfast, lunch, and tea,
For they are hungry men;
But different folk have different views;
I know a person small –
She keeps ten million serving-men,
Who get no rest at all!
She sends 'em abroad on her own affairs
From the second she opens her eyes –
One million Hows, two million Wheres,
And seven million Whys![45]

6

THE SING-SONG OF OLD MAN KANGAROO

Not always was the Kangaroo as now we do behold him, but a Different Animal with four short legs. He was grey and he was woolly, and his pride was inordinate; he danced on an outcrop in the middle of Australia, and he went to the Little God Nqa.[1]

The caption to this image tells us that 'This is a picture of Old Man Kangaroo when he was the Different Animal with four short legs. I have drawn him grey and woolly, and you can see that he is very proud because he has a wreath of flowers in his hair.' Time and place are exact. Old Man Kangaroo is dancing before Nqa 'in the middle of Australia at six o'clock before breakfast'. A further detail is that 'The Kangaroo hasn't any real name except Boomer. He lost it because he was so proud.'[2] *Pride* caused him to *lose his name*? The tone of this nonsensical statement achieves the impossible: it allows us to feel that the loss of his name was natural and inevitable.

He went to Nqa at six before breakfast, saying 'Make me different from all other animals by five this afternoon.' Up jumped Nqa from his seat on the sand-flat and shouted, 'Go away!' He was grey and he was woolly, and his pride was inordinate: he danced on a rock-ledge in the middle of Australia, and he went to the Middle God Nquing. He went to Nquing at eight after breakfast, saying, 'Make me different from all other animals; make me, also, wonderfully popular by five

84

this afternoon.' Up jumped Nquing from his burrow in the spinifex and shouted, 'Go away!' He was grey and he was woolly, and his pride was inordinate: he danced on a sandbank in the middle of Australia, and he went to the Big God Nquong. He went to Nquong at ten before dinner-time, saying, 'Make me different from all other animals; make me popular and wonderfully run after by five this afternoon.'

Up jumped Nquong from his bath in the salt-pan and shouted, 'Yes, I will!'

Nquong called Dingo – Yellow-Dog Dingo – always hungry, dusty in the sunshine, and showed him Kangaroo. Nquong said, 'Dingo! Wake up Dingo! Do you see that gentleman dancing on an ashpit? He wants to be popular and very truly run after. Dingo, make him so!'

Up jumped Dingo – Yellow-Dog Dingo – and said, 'What, *that* cat-rabbit?'

Off ran Dingo – Yellow-Dog Dingo – always hungry, grinning like a coal-scuttle, – ran after Kangaroo.

Off went the proud Kangaroo on his four little legs like a bunny.

This, O Beloved of mine, ends the first part of the tale![3]

The 'Sing-Song' of Old Man Kangaroo is printed as prose but sounds like blank verse.* It has the energy and impetus of Whitman's free-verse metre in *Leaves of Grass*. This and the inventive similes propel the story forward.

'Be careful what you wish for' could have been the subtitle for this story, as also for 'The Elephant's Child' which has just preceded it. In that story the answer to the Child's question – 'what does the Crocodile have for dinner?' – is 'Elephant's Child', and in the Kangaroo story the granting of Old Man Kangaroo's wish to be 'very truly run after' is achieved by making him the potential dinner of the always hungry Yellow-Dog Dingo. Dingo is a wonderfully vivid character. Teasing and enigmatic, the 'Big God Nquong' could have been imagined as having the authority and sculptural calm of Baviaan from 'How the Leopard got his Spots'. Baviaan seems as impersonal as the Sphinx, and Quong could have been invested with a similar degree of dignity, mystery and cultural remoteness. But this is the Australian outback as Kipling imagined it, where manners

---

* In the *Just so* manuscript the kangaroo does actually sing, as well as dance, when he visits the three gods.[4]

are rough and direct – matey, indeed – so the Big God Nquong in his bath could be a version of one of Kipling's working-class heroes from *Soldiers Three* (1888): a mythologised Mulvaney, naked, bearded, uncouth and hairy, while retaining undeniable strength and authority.

Yellow-Dog Dingo and Old Man Kangaroo are caught in a pattern where the gap between predator and prey never closes, with Yellow-Dog 'grinning like a coal-scuttle', 'grinning like a rat-trap', 'grinning like a horse-collar, never getting nearer'. Pursuer and pursued are challenged by a river, and at that point the kangaroo's characteristic legs begin to grow. The chase continues:

> Never getting nearer, never getting farther; and they came to the Wollgong River. Now, there wasn't any bridge, and there wasn't any ferry-boat, and Kangaroo didn't know how to get over; so he stood on his legs and hopped. He had to! He hopped through the Flinders; he hopped through the Cinders; he hopped through the deserts in the middle of Australia. He hopped like a Kangaroo. First he hopped one yard; then he hopped three yards; then he hopped five yards; his legs growing stronger; his legs growing longer. He hadn't any time for rest or refreshment, and he wanted them very much.[5]

Yellow-Dog Dingo wonders: 'what in the world or out of it made Old Man Kangaroo hop. For he hopped like a cricket; like a pea in a saucepan; or a new rubber ball on a nursery floor. He had to! He tucked up his front legs; he hopped on his hind legs; he stuck out his tail for a balance-weight behind him; and he hopped through the Darling Downs. He had to!'[6] (The rubber ball on the nursery floor reminds us of the close intimacy between Kipling and his child audience as he tells his story.)

As evening approaches Nquong comes out of his bath in the salt-pans to point out to Kangaroo that the challenge is completed. 'Then said Nquong, who is always a gentleman, "Why aren't you grateful to Yellow-Dog Dingo? Why don't you thank him for all he has done for you?"'

Kangaroo protests, and Nquong reminds him of the terms: 'Didn't you ask me to make you different from all other animals, as well as to make you very truly sought after? And now it is five o'clock.'[7]

Kipling was probably echoing bush ballads that he had heard among the settlers in Australia, and he knew the popular Sydney ballad writer A.B. 'Banjo' Paterson, famous especially for 'Waltzing Matilda' which was written and first performed in 1895. Each of the reactions of the three gods in the Australian desert can be sung to its tune. 'Up jumped Nqa from his seat on the sand-flat', 'Up jumped Nquing from his burrow in the spinifex', 'Up jumped Nquong from his bath in the salt-pan': these lines echo the sturdy nihilistic defiance of the Swagman's end in the ballad:

> Up jumped the swagman and sprang into the billabong,
> 'You'll never take me alive' said he,
> And his ghost may be heard as you pass by that billabong,
> 'Who'll come a-waltzing Matilda with me?'

A little later Paterson and Kipling briefly collaborated. Early in 1900 Kipling went out to South Africa to support the British Army in their war against the Boers. In March, Lord Roberts, who was in charge of the British offensive (and a friend of Kipling), established an army newspaper, probably the first of its kind in military history, and asked Kipling to edit and contribute to it. For this short-lived journal, Paterson, who was also then in South Africa, wrote spirited ballads which were as popular with the British troops as Kipling's own contributions.[8] Paterson had been described in the press as the 'Australian Kipling'. From his perspective Paterson saw in Kipling a 'quick, nervous energy [...] his talk is a gabble, a chatter, a constant jumping from one point to another. In manner, he is more like a businessman than a literary celebrity. There is nothing of the dreamer about him.' He found Kipling a double personality ('Jekyll and Hyde'), simultaneously a politician and a writer. 'He yarned away about shoes and ships and sealing-wax and cabbages and kings; interested in everything; jumping from one subject to another, from his residence in New York to border battles on the Indian frontier; from the necessity of getting your local colour right, to the difficulty of getting a good illustrator.' And he put his finger on a key aspect of Kipling, his chameleon's ability to adapt to any new setting in which he found himself: 'you could have dumped Kipling down in a splitter's camp in the back-blocks of Australia and he would have been quite at home; and would have gone away, leaving the impression that he was a decent sort of bloke that asked a lot of questions.'[9] The two men clearly got on famously.

Kipling had visited Australia in 1891, only for two weeks and in the developed cities of Sydney and Melbourne, with a brief visit to Adelaide and a stop at Hobart in Tasmania. He never went back, but retained an interest in and enthusiasm for Australia and its settlers. He may have known a story in K.L. Parker's *Australian Legendary Tales* (1896) in which a four-legged kangaroo (which at first looks like a dog) joins an Aboriginal tribal dance. The kangaroo ends the dance on his hind legs with his tail sticking out behind him. As a penalty for his intrusion he is made to remain in that posture for ever.

The unfolding plot of Kipling's Kangaroo story turns on wordplay. The Kangaroo seeks to be 'wonderfully run after' (by which he means 'much admired'). Instead, as we have seen, he is literally 'run after' by the Dingo until both creatures are hungry and exhausted. He has full kangaroo legs as a result, but his complaint is that he had expected charms and incantations and all he got was a practical joke in the form of a severe physical challenge. The enigmatic tale also ends in an impasse. Kangaroo and Dingo both ask Nquong an urgent nursery question: 'what may I have for my tea?' Nquong replies, 'Come and ask me about it tomorrow, because I'm going to wash.' So the two creatures are left hungry in the middle of Australia, and each says to the other: 'That's *your* fault.'[10]

The theme compares with similar patterns in some of Kipling's adult stories: the mutual recrimination and blocked ambition of two British

The caption to this image tells us that Old Man Kangaroo also has a pouch: 'He had to have a pouch just as he had to have legs.'[11] A detail not explained in the caption is that it has 'Patent Fed Govt Aus' (Patent Federal Government of Australia) written across it: in other words, it has been patented, as an exclusive attribute of the kangaroo as a species – a joke that would certainly need to be explained to the child audience.[12]

adventurers lead to stalemate and death in 'The Man who would be King' (in *The Phantom Rickshaw*, 1888; this story is discussed in conjunction with 'The Butterfly that Stamped' in chapter 12). The narrative dead-end of the Kangaroo story also invites comparison (surprising though this may seem) with the mystifying ending of one of Kipling's most sophisticated narratives, 'Mrs Bathurst', in *Traffics and Discoveries* (1904).* 'Mrs Bathurst' closes with two corpses, only one of whom, Vickery, is identified. Vickery was a British naval officer who had deserted his ship because of his sexual obsession with a Mrs Bathurst, based on a New Zealand widow who worked behind a bar; in *Something of Myself* Kipling thought that he recalled her from Auckland, but in New Zealand there is an alternative tradition which has her working behind a bar in Christchurch. The dead figures, Vickery and his unknown companion, have been struck by lightning near a railway line outside Bulawayo (in modern Zimbabwe, which was then Southern Rhodesia). How they came to be there, and who the second figure is, remain indeterminable (and also the subject of a number of ingenious suggestions).[16]

The message of 'The Sing-Song of Old Man Kangaroo' is that it is a mistake to seek popularity; the need for adulation in the playground is the error of a small child. We are reminded that the young Kipling had desperately needed to draw attention to himself. As a very small boy, before the Southsea years, he was recorded as marching down the street shouting 'Ruddy is coming! An *angry* Ruddy is coming.' (This was during a visit to his mother's sister, Louisa Baldwin,† at Bewdley in Staffordshire.)[17] But the

---

*'Mrs Bathurst' has been exhaustively discussed by academic critics. One reading of it, which seems to me both accessible and plausible, is offered by Elliot L. Gilbert in *The Good Kipling* (1972).[13] He makes a felicitous comparison with one of the *Just so Stories* when he says that casual readers of Kipling are 'always surprised to learn that the author of "How the Camel Got his Hump" is also the creator of some of the most doggedly inexplicable fictions written in the twentieth century'.[14] He invites us to see 'Mrs Bathurst' as an early 'modernist' text which is comparable with some of the narrative experiments in Joyce's *Ulysses* (1922).[15]

† Aunt Louisa's son Stanley Baldwin, one of Kipling's favourite cousins when they were children, would later become Prime Minister. The adult Kipling was unable to agree with the politics of the adult Stanley Baldwin.

older Kipling had also been 'run after' in a different way. In the miserable year of 1896, when Kipling brought his charge of assault against Beatty Balestier, he had found the court case a 'nightmare' and an 'atrocious affair'. The glare of hostile publicity and mockery horrified him. Being hounded by the American gutter press was an intensely unwelcome form of fame, and the sharp understanding that fame is a double-edged sword would have been brought home to him by this humiliating experience.[18]

The story of Old Man Kangaroo is in effect told twice, first in the Whitmanesque free verse which takes up the body of the whole tale, and secondly in the tightly rhyming and vigorously headlong poem which ends the story:

This is the mouth-filling song
Of the race that was run by a Boomer,
Run in a single burst – only event of its kind –
Started by Big God Nquong from Warrigaborrigarooma,
Old Man Kangaroo first: Yellow-Dog Dingo behind.

Kangaroo bounded away,
His back-legs working like pistons –
Bounded from morning till dark,
Twenty-five feet to a bound.
Yellow-Dog Dingo lay
Like a yellow cloud in the distance –
Much too busy to bark.
My! but they covered the ground!

Nobody knows where they went,
Or followed the track that they flew in,
For that Continent
Hadn't been given a name.
They ran thirty degrees,

The Sing-Song of Old Man Kangaroo

From Torres Straits to the Leeuwin
(Look at the Atlas, please),
And they ran back as they came.

S'posing you could trot
From Adelaide to the Pacific,
For an afternoon's run –
Half what these gentlemen did –
You would feel rather hot,
But your legs would develop terrific –
Yes, my importunate son,
You'd be a Marvellous Kid!![19]

The close of this poem anticipates the most famous of all Kipling's poems, 'If –', written in 1910 and ending:

If you can fill the unforgiving minute
With sixty seconds' worth of distance run,
Yours is the Earth and everything that's in it,
And – which is more – you'll be a Man, my son!

The whole story was written probably in August 1899 and the marvellous kid must be Kipling's son, John, born in 1897. John would have been only 3 when the story was first published (in the *Ladies' Home Journal* in 1900); he would have enjoyed the pictures and the rhythmical insistence of the narrative.

As he grew older, John's relationship with his father was developed through the letters Kipling sent to him while he was away at boarding school. Kipling loved creating inventive, funny, sesquipedalian letters: they rejoice in long learned words which would prompt questions in an intrigued and delighted child. Some of them turn the whole family's interaction into a kind of social comedy scripted by Oscar Wilde (though Kipling would not have welcomed that comparison). His letters about

Carrie's illnesses are in this vein. Carrie suffered from (often non-specific) physical complaints which became steadily worse after 1900. Kipling wrote bulletins of her health to the children which turned the ailments into farce. The comedy is playful though, not brutal, and full of affection for Carrie; Kipling's motivation was to keep his children informed without worrying them. On 15 July 1908 he wrote to Elsie, 'you may have noticed that on Saturday and Sunday I was, as your dear French governess says, *deestray* – which is pure French for absorbed and worried'. The worry was caused by 'your Mummy's pains in her inside'. She 'sat about and imagined the various diseases that the pains might mean. She counted up to 97 of them – or three. I forget which.'

Kipling took Carrie to see his friend Sir John Bland-Sutton, the London physician who treated the couple throughout this period.

> He punched and he whacked and he thumped her and did all those things which are necessary when one has a tummy, and he wound up by saying that there was nothing wrong with Mummy in the way of the five or six terrible diseases she had imagined herself to possess. She has *not* got Squiffamalosis, or Ventritis or lumps or bumps or other things. 'Then what has she got?' says I. 'Well, she's got a delicate alimentary canal,' says he (this is doctorese for indigestion).[20]

Elsie was now an intelligent and observant 12-year-old, well able to laugh indulgently with her father over his management of her mother. Bland-Sutton prescribed 'a simple but loathsome medicine of one's childhood – nothing less or more than CASTOR OIL! When we got out into Bond Street and I wanted to dance in the puddles (it was raining) Mummy was furious!'

> I said things about not working after meals and getting indigestion and resting when one was tired. It was all quite true and improving, and she was quite mad with me. But no matter. [...] Today she is vastly better because she knows she has not got the 97 separate and fatal diseases which she thought she had.[21]

The Sing-Song of Old Man Kangaroo

The *Just so Stories* were scripts written for performance, with Kipling himself as the performing voice. Kipling adopts a performing identity for himself in this letter to Elsie:

> Dear Bird, The house is four times emptier and five times larger than it was at 11 o'clock this morning. Can it be possible, said Mr Campbell, that the departure of a F-t P-rs-n in a pony-cart has had anything do to with this surprising change?

The Fat Person in the pony-cart is Elsie herself, while 'Mr Campbell' is an alternative persona that Kipling often adopted in his letters to his children if he was giving advice: 'If you ever feel doubtful about your conduct, you have only to write and I myself will instruct you further, said Mr Campbell.'[22] He wants to distance himself from the pomposity of a Polonius and at the same time he *does* want the children to learn life-skills from his letters.

More of the letters are to John than to Elsie, the obvious reason being that John was away at boarding schools from 1907. Initially, aged 10, he was sent to a preparatory school called St Aubyn's, close to the Burne-Jones' home in Rottingdean, and later, from September 1911, to Wellington College, many of whose boys were destined for the army. John Kipling's eyesight was so poor that he was unsuited to this kind of school, but his academic results were not strong enough for him to be admitted to Eton, which was the other option in Kipling's mind. After Wellington, John was send to a 'crammer', a tutorial college which prepared boys for admission to Sandhurst. 'Crammers' are often referred to in *Stalky & Co.*

Kipling's love for his only son was combined with anxious pride in his achievements and a good deal of kindly, if exasperated, comment on his shortcomings (his inability to spell accurately, his failure to get higher than bottom of the class in maths, and so on). When John was due to leave his preparatory school and go on to Wellington Kipling visited the place and sent a long descriptive letter, with drawings, to encourage him to feel positive about this next stage: 'It's a simply glorious building with huge iron gates and quadrangles and inner courtyards standing in the middle of the most splendid grounds that ever you saw. The cricket and football fields are a dream of delight.' The letter goes on in the same enthusiastic vein, somewhat overselling the school; Wellington has some military-looking formal buildings and attractive grounds, but it is not a beautiful place. 'The School Chapel is about three times the size of Rottingdean Church. It holds 500 boys. [...] Pearson's House seems *very* delightful. There are about 30 chaps in it. They have each a cubicle to work and sleep in – with a big couch, desk, chair and any amount of knickknacks on the walls.' Kipling includes drawings of the cubicles.[23] There is anxiety in his mind here about 'beastliness', by which he meant sexual activity among the boys at the school; this probably recalls his own rage when he learnt that during his time at the United Services College, Westward Ho!, he had himself been suspected of the same thing. Later, when John was in his teens, Kipling wrote a touchingly anxious father's letter. John had just gone back to school and Kipling had been laid up with a heavy cold. 'What really bothered me most was not being able to have a last jaw with you. I wanted to tell you a lot of things about keeping clear of any chap who is even suspected of beastliness.' Maybe John had been showing too much interest in a particular boy, because Kipling's warning becomes a bit more specific: 'Whatever their merits may be in the athletic line they are at heart only sweeps and scum and *all* friendship or acquaintance with them ends in sorrow and disgrace.'[24] Kipling was doing what he saw as a father's duty here, and doing it well by the standards of his class and time; many Edwardian fathers would have found it simply impossible to raise this topic. But a sad gulf has opened up between this anxious communication with his adolescent son and the open and playful narrative voice speaking to small children in the *Just so Stories*.

7

THE BEGINNING OF THE ARMADILLOES

This, O Best Beloved, is another story of the High and Far-Off Times. In the very middle of those times was a Stickly-Prickly Hedgehog, and he lived on the banks of the turbid Amazon, eating shelly snails and things. And he had a friend, a Slow-Solid Tortoise, who lived on the banks of the turbid Amazon, eating green lettuces and things. And so *that* was all right, Best Beloved. Do you see?

But also, and at the same time, in those High and Far-Off Times, there was a Painted Jaguar, and he lived on the banks of the turbid Amazon too; and he ate everything that he could catch. When he could not catch deer or monkeys he would eat frogs and beetles; and when he could not catch frogs and beetles he went to his Mother Jaguar, and she told him how to eat hedgehogs and tortoises. She said to him ever so many times, graciously waving her tail, 'My son, when you find a Hedgehog you must drop him into the water and then he will uncoil, and when you catch a Tortoise you must scoop him out of his shell with your paw.' And so that was all right, Best Beloved.

One beautiful night on the banks of the turbid Amazon, Painted Jaguar found Stickly-Prickly Hedgehog and Slow-Solid Tortoise sitting under the trunk of a fallen tree. They could not run away, and so Stickly-Prickly curled himself up into a ball, because he was a Hedgehog, and Slow-Solid Tortoise drew in his head and feet into his shell as far as they would go, because he was a Tortoise; and so *that* was all right, Best Beloved. Do you see?[1]

Like 'The Elephant's Child', this tale is again set in 'High and Far-Off Times'. The two phrases addressed to the small child, 'that was all right' and 'Do you see?', become refrains in this story, recurring as a pattern throughout its text. Indeed, Kipling's attention to pattern, design, repetition and the look of the text and its accompanying illustrations are particularly striking features of this story.

The Painted Jaguar is young and easily misled by the Tortoise and the Hedgehog, who give him carefully garbled versions of his mother's instructions. The poor young Jaguar is lost:

> 'When you scoop water with your paw you uncoil it with a Hedgehog,' said Stickly-Prickly. 'Remember that, because it's important.'
>
> '*But*,' said the Tortoise, 'when you paw your meat you drop it into a Tortoise with a scoop. Why can't you understand?'[2]

The comedy builds, the Jaguar is hopelessly confused and we, like Kipling's child audience, are delighted by the nonsensical variations on the original advice. We are by now familiar with the idiom of the stories, and have heard the tales 'explaining' how the Elephant, Camel, Kangaroo, Leopard and Rhinoceros arrived at their present appearance. This pattern, the repetition with variation of his plot devices, is an important part of the pleasure given by Kipling's own readings.

Many of Joel Chandler Harris's *Uncle Remus* stories are about Brer Fox's attempts to catch and eat Brer Rabbit. In the best-known tale, 'Brer Rabbit and the Tar-Baby', the rabbit is trapped when it gets stuck to Brer Fox's tar-baby. He escapes by saying that of all the punishments he can imagine, the very worst would be to be thrown into the briar patch, whereupon Brer Fox (rather easily outwitted, it may be felt) does precisely that. The story ends with the rabbit exulting at a distance and chanting that he was 'born and bred in a briar patch' and therefore Brer Fox has thrown him into exactly the environment that suits him best. As a schoolboy in Devon Kipling had read Harris's *Uncle Remus* stories. He wrote to Harris in December 1895: 'I wonder if you could realize how Uncle Remus his sayings and the sayings of the noble beasties ran like wild fire through an English public school when I was about fifteen.' 'I remember', he added, 'the bodily heaving into a furze-bush of a young fag solely because his nickname had been "Rabbit" before the tales invaded the school and – well, we assumed that he ought to have been "born an' bred in a briar-patch".'[3]

The device in the Armadillo story resembles Brer Rabbit's deception of Brer Fox. The ways in which the Tortoise and the Hedgehog outwit the young Painted Jaguar are also not unlike the ways in which the residents of Study Number 5 in *Stalky & Co.* confound their adversaries. Cooperation and common purpose are the keys to their success, and a further important bond is their low status in the United Services College. The stories place them in the middle of the school, well below the young tyrants appointed as 'prefects', who enjoy vigorously defended privileges (the right to smoke, for example, and the right to beat the junior boys for such offences as missing football matches). The skill with which Tortoise and Hedgehog outwit the young Jaguar has a strong feel of the lower form boys in *Stalky & Co.* successfully plotting against the petty authority of their schoolmasters and occasionally (as, especially, in a story called 'The Moral Reformers') against bullying by the older boys.

The fact that his son John would have to go through the rigours and rituals of British middle-class education would have been in Kipling's mind as he invented the callow and easily deceived Painted Jaguar and his poised and socially polished mother. Painted Jaguar can be imagined as a public schoolboy from Eton or Winchester, good-looking, well presented and overprotected, whose mother guides him and sees that he makes mistakes and needs to be set on the right path.[4] The Tortoise and the Hedgehog are like the boys in Kipling's study at the United Services College, neither rich nor well-born but wily and canny in their dealings with authority.

The Painted Jaguar is outwitted because the Tortoise and the Hedgehog vary his mother's instructions ('are you sure of what your Mummy told you?') until they trick him into letting them escape. The story then adds a further layer of threat: the Painted Jaguar, following further advice from his mother, invents a mnemonic: 'Can't curl but can swim – Slow-Solid, that's him! Curls up but can't swim – Stickly-Prickly, that's him!' His prey recognise the seriousness of this: '"He'll never forget that this month of Sundays," said Stickly-Prickly. "Hold up my chin, Slow-and-Solid. I'm going to try to learn to swim. It may be useful." '[5] The animals pool their physical characteristics to become a new species, and the Painted Jaguar runs petulantly to his mother once more: 'it isn't a Hedgehog, and it isn't a Tortoise. It's a little bit of both, and I don't know its proper name.' Mother, unsurprisingly, is imperious and arbitrary in reply: 'Everything has its proper name. I should call it "Armadillo" till I found out the real one.'[6] This moment in the story has the confident registration of random particularity which is characteristic of dream narratives. Why 'Armadillo'? There is no explanation of this.

The narrative voice ends the story confidently saying: 'There are Hedgehogs and Tortoises in other places, of course (there are some in my garden); but the real old and clever kind, with their scales lying lippety-lappety one over the other, like pine-cone scales, that lived on the banks of the turbid Amazon in the High and Far-Off Days, are always called Armadillos, because they were so clever.' This is followed by the friendly child-centred refrain which forces us to feel that it is the *only* possible explanation: 'So *that's* all right, Best Beloved. Do you see?'[7] This coinage is certainly not 'all right' in the sense of having been arrived at by any kind of rational process, but the arbitrariness is the point. 'Armadillos' and 'clever' have become firmly linked in the reader's sense of what is apt.

All the captions to the images in the *Just so Stories* contribute to the narratives, but in the Armadillo story Kipling takes this much further than in the other tales. He clearly became intrigued by the challenge of creating his 'map of the Turbid Amazon'.[8] The captions to his map comprise a complete secondary narrative. Ingenuity and play for their own sake have taken over here as though Kipling is back to his childhood self, creating ingenious solitary games to alleviate the boredom and terror of Mrs Holloway's house in Southsea. The main narrative of the Armadillo story belongs to the 'very middle' of the 'High and Far-Off Times'. To this extent it is like 'The Elephant's Child', which is also set at a midpoint in the history of evolution as Kipling has imagined it. In the alternative Genesis that Kipling has invented (with its nod to the Lamarckian theory of the development of species) the skill with which the two creatures transform themselves into armadillos belongs to the 'High and Far-Off Times' at which the world was created.

The caption begins: 'This is an inciting map of the Turbid Amazon done in Red and Black. It hasn't anything to do with the story except that there are two Armadilloes in it – up by the top. The inciting part are the adventures that happened to the men who went along the road marked in red.'[9] (The colour is seen at its best in the 1937 'Sussex' edition of Kipling's works.) Kipling did not know Brazil (and would not visit that country until 1927) but he devised here a mythical 'old' map of the Amazon with a complete account of the adventures of a fictional English sailor exploring the river in 1503. The plate showing the map includes a detailed travel narrative which imitates the Elizabethan English of Richard Hakluyt, the scholar and diplomat who promoted the colonising of America. Kipling owned a set of his *Principall Navigations, Voiages, Traffiques and Discoveries of the English Nation* (1598–1600). (Kipling recalled this when he chose *Traffics and Discoveries* as the title for his 1904 collection of short stories.)

Kipling's plate gives an illustration of the Amazon River with a mass of scrolls superimposed on it. They set out the story of a ship fitted out by 'Sir Mat Vows' (or 'Matt Vowse'; the story gives variant spellings) which left Bristol on 17 April 1503, on a mission of 'ranke follie', a 'wavery and lamentable voyage towards ye E Indies'. It left with 57 men and returned to Bristol with only 11. This introduction is followed by a series of scrolls which when read in sequence are in effect the ship's log recording the whole trip. Apart from its setting on the Amazon and a brief reference to

an encounter ashore with a creature referred to as 'Armourdilla or Hog-in-harnesse' (Sir Mat's phrase for the Armadillo),[10] there is no close connection with the main narrative. Like the digressions in Sterne's *Tristram Shandy* (1759–67), the story of Sir Mat shares its own inventiveness with the delighted reader. This is the only *Just so* story in which the embedded narrative in one of the images comprises an additional and different story. The juxtaposition and intermingling of these diverse narrative forms can be taken as Kipling's reflection on the nature of an armadillo itself, which in the story is half mammal and half reptile.

The reader experiences two narratives: the dramatic interplay between the obstreperous and foolish young jaguar, his over-gracious and controlling mother, and the skill with which the Tortoise and the Hedgehog outwit their murderous designs; and the tale of the sixteenth-century sea-going adventurer mapping out an unfamiliar part of the earth and suffering in the process. The two narratives display admiration for ingenuity and stubbornness, and a delight in imaginative armchair exploration of a distant place at a remote time. A striking feature of the map is an illustrated story, top centre. It shows a white European man being worshipped by black men, and has this inscription: 'Sir Matt. Vowse having put on hys back & front pieces [of armour] after cleansing of 'em brighte was here worship as a Pagod by divers silie Indians.' Sir Mat's adventure here with the 'silly Indians' could be a recall of 'The Man who would be King', where Dravot and Carnehan, rogue adventurers, become objects of veneration in a remote community. The story of Sir Mat and his crew is a discrete entity within the Armadillo story, and the literary pleasure for the reader involves accepting the coexistence of these wholly distinct art forms within the pages of a single short tale.

The second illustration to the main narrative compresses the Armadillo story into a single image. The Tortoise and the Hedgehog are taking on each other's characteristics while the Painted Jaguar watches, one of his paws 'carefully tied up by his mother, because he pricked himself scooping the Hedgehog'. Kipling's caption tells us that 'This is a

picture of the whole story of the Jaguar and the Hedgehog and the Tortoise *and* the Armadillo all in a heap. It looks rather the same any way you turn it.' He adds: 'It is all a magic picture, that is one of the reasons why I haven't drawn the Jaguar's whiskers. The other reason was that he was so young that his whiskers had not grown. The Jaguar's pet name with his Mummy was Doffles.'[11] This image is contained within a circle, like a medallion, and offers as much visual pleasure as the invented map.

One of the story's themes is that cooperation is the best way to ensure the survival of individuals. There is some thematic resemblance here, I think, to one of Kipling's most accomplished mature short stories, 'The

Bridge-Builders' (collected in *The Day's Work*, 1898), which tells the story of two young British men, seasoned civil engineer Findlayson and his assistant and closest colleague Hitchcock, who supervise the building of a major bridge across the Ganges. It is a strong example of a narrative about the value of cooperation and common purpose. The two young men comprise a kind of human equivalent of the Tortoise and the Hedgehog, who work together so efficiently to ensure their own survival in the Armadillo story. It also combines direct and carefully noted realism with magical invention of the kind that characterises the talking animal stories in the two *Jungle Books*. The British built several major bridges across Indian rivers. The Sutlej bridge, also known as the 'Empress' Bridge (in honour of Queen Victoria, who was by this time Empress of India), was built in 1887, and was part of the British transport network which brought together the disparate regions of the Indian subcontinent. An equally important structure, the Dufferin Bridge, was built to cross the Ganges. It carried the Grand Trunk Road (a central symbol in Kipling's *Kim*). It was named after Lord Dufferin, Governor-General of India, who became particularly friendly with the Kipling family.

Kipling's story celebrates the achievements of two young men whose success in the construction of the bridge depends on their mutual confidence and their joint authority:

> None knew better than these two [Findlayson and Hitchcock], who trusted each other, how the underlings were not to be trusted. They had been tried many times in sudden crises – by slipping of booms, by breaking of tackle, failure of cranes, and wrath of the river – but no stress had brought to light any man among them whom Findlayson and Hitchcock would have honoured by working as remorselessly as they worked themselves.[12]

The bridge they are building is threatened with destruction by flood and Findlayson is overcome by fever. One of the central figures in the story, a highly competent Indian named Peroo, persuades him to take opium. As a consequence Findlayson has an opium-induced dream, one of Kipling's most developed imaginative explorations of visionary experience, in which the Hindu gods hold a conversation, or *punchayet*, about the threat represented by the bridge. *Punchayet* is clearly a word which pleased Kipling: he uses it for the council of animals who meet to discuss the Camel's laziness in his Camel tale. The Hindu gods are based on a trinity comprising Brahm (the dreamer whose dream comprises the whole act of creation), Vishnu the protector and Siva the destroyer. Kipling's own favourites included Ganesh the Elephant god, whom Kipling adopted as his own emblem (Ganesh was a manifestation of Siva), and Krishna, the young male god who loves humans, a manifestation of Vishnu (and who is in later Hinduism the master of all the other gods); the physical beauty of Krishna can be imagined as one of Lockwood Kipling's many visual realisations of Mowgli as an idealised adolescent in the *Jungle Books*.

The gods in their *punchayet* predict that attitudes to them in India will change, but that they as gods will continue. The changes will be major but not final. Krishna's extended speech about the nature of adaptation makes this clear:

Me alone they cannot kill, so long as maiden and man meet together or the spring follows the winter rains. Heavenly Ones, not for nothing have I walked upon the earth. My people know not now what they know; but I, who live with them, I read their hearts. Great Kings, the beginning of the end is born already. The fire-carriages shout the names of new Gods that are *not* the old under new names. Drink now and eat greatly! Bathe your faces in the smoke of the altars before they grow cold! Take dues and listen to the cymbals and the drums, Heavenly Ones, while yet there are flowers and songs. As men count time the end is far off; but as we who know reckon it is today. I have spoken.[13]

Kipling clearly endorses Krishna's humanism as he defends the Indian people. Mankind is punished by the flood for daring to violate the Ganges. Humans, Krishna says, are '*My* people – who lie under the leaf-roofs of the village yonder – [...] the young girls, and the young men who sing to them in the dark – [...] the child that will be born next morn – [...and] that which was begotten tonight.'[14] This dream sequence invites us into an experiment in perspective, where timeless and universal reality reduces the local activity of building a bridge to minuscule size and significance. This does not mean that it is subordinated to the world of the gods. Krishna tells his fellow gods that the modern engineering works will reduce the gods to 'rag-Gods, pot Godlings of the tree, and the village mark'. But Indra challenges this by saying that both gods and men are the dream of Brahm. 'Be content. Brahm dreams still. The dreams come and go, and the nature of the dreams changes, but still Brahm dreams.'[15]

Elliot L. Gilbert wrote persuasively about the imaginative wholeness of 'The Bridge-Builders', speaking of the 'delicate shading of the world of reality into the world of dreams'. To his mind, the coexistence of the imaginative and the real in the story 'contains no shock at all':

> Instead, the real world blends so imperceptibly into the world of the supernatural – steam engines and talking elephants exist so comfortably side by side – that for all the violent contrasts inherent in the subject matter of the story, the reader often has the sense of viewing not two worlds but one. This, of course, is precisely Kipling's point; that the India of which he writes – the India of this very special instant of history – stands between two ways of life in a world of its own, a world in which [...] a man may at one moment pray to a river, the next to the dome of a cathedral, and the next to a low-press cylinder in an engine room.[16]

I experience the same sense of viewing not two worlds but one when reading 'The Beginning of the Armadilloes'. Kipling's 'venturesome adventures' in the 'inciting map of the Amazon' coexist with the story of the cooperation between the Tortoise and the Hedgehog in a way which is simultaneously wholly satisfying and logically inexplicable. 'The Bridge-Builders' – a rich narrative which is both about the value of common purpose and cooperation and about the coexistence of the supernatural and the real – shares the elaborate inventiveness with which the Armadillo story has been constructed. The impossible is made possible. Two sharply contrasting species become a single new animal, and two sharply contrasting kinds of narrative – the talking animal story and the seventeenth-century adventure story contained in the map – fold into one another to become a single form of pleasure for the reader. The story of the Armadilloes closes with a quite different kind of literary experience, a poem which has the rhythms and exuberance of a sea-shanty and speaks to any adventurous child. The second verse of this song runs:

> I've never seen a Jaguar
>   Nor yet an Armadill –
> O dilloing in his armour,
>   And I s'pose I never will,
> Unless I go to Rio
>
>   These wonders to behold –
> Roll down – roll down to Rio
> Roll really down to Rio!
> Oh, I'd love to roll to Rio
>   Some day before I'm old![17]

In one sense the 'Beginning' of the Armadilloes is not a beginning but an end. In the stories that succeed this one Kipling chose to change his focus. The first seven stories, the tales of the Whale, Camel, Rhinoceros, Leopard, Elephant, Kangaroo and Armadilloes, have a self-evident community of theme. They are evolutionary fables giving magical or mythical versions of development for each of these creatures. 'The Story of the Armadilloes' is the pivot, or point of turn, in this sequence. It is the last of the stories to offer a version of how a species began.

The Beginning of the Armadilloes

In the following stories the focus moves away from the development of species to other forms of early history. 'How the First Letter was Written' and 'How the Alphabet was Made' are directly linked with each other in their playful accounts of Stone Age man and his social order and communication skills. The three stories that completed the 1902 volume – 'The Crab that Played with the Sea', 'The Cat that Walked by Himself' and 'The Butterfly that Stamped' – further explore the power of creation myths and the origins of selected human institutions. The two stories published after 1902, 'The Tabu Tale' and 'Ham and the Porcupine', bring the whole tally up to fourteen stories.

In his 1977 biography of Kipling, Angus Wilson was firmly discriminating in his treatment of the *Just so Stories*; for him the first seven stories were the 'cream of the collection', and the remaining stories represented a falling-off. He had further reservations: he thought that the 'pleasing little Darwinian send-up that unites these first seven and best stories was lost altogether on Kipling's and other children', and that 'sentimental whimsicality takes over' when we have the stories of man's advancement, the stories about the first letter, the development of the alphabet, the domestication of animals by humans in a cave and so on.[18] My own view is that if there is any falling-off it is into the temptation to end a story with boisterous laughter. This causes the eighth story, 'How the First Letter was Written', to feel less fully and richly imagined than the first seven stories.

Stone Age man is treated as fantasy in the *Just so Stories*, and similarly the Romans who lived in Britain are treated as fantasy material in poems and stories from *Puck of Pook's Hill* (1906) and *Rewards and Fairies* (1910). The frame setting for these stories is Bateman's, the Kiplings' home in Sussex from 1902 onwards. 'A Centurion of the Thirtieth' is the story of a fine-looking Roman soldier who comes into the children's garden and into their lives from the fourth century, a late stage in the Roman occupation of Britain when the Roman legions were leaving their western empire and Christianity was competing with such cults as the worship of Mithras (popular among the Roman soldiers who were still defending Hadrian's Wall). Kipling's children John and Elsie are given the names 'Dan' and 'Una'. Puck, from Shakespeare's *A Midsummer Night's Dream*, is the intermediary who brings figures from the past into Dan and Una's lives.

Kipling's stories about Puck and the Edwardian children whom he visits bear some comparison with the near-contemporary stories by E. Nesbit in *Five Children and It* (1902), *The Phoenix and the Carpet* (1904) and *The Story of the Amulet* (1906), though in Nesbit's stories the rules governing time travel are more fluid. In Nesbit's stories, the children can visit the remote past: Atlantis at the moment of its destruction, for example, or a forgotten stronghold full of treasure during the wars of medieval France. In Kipling's Puck stories, figures from the past can enter the present inhabited by Dan and Una, but the children themselves are fixed in their Edwardian setting (based on their garden at Bateman's).

The *Just so Stories* of 1902 is a completely satisfying masterpiece, a perfectly managed work of art where the stories, poems and images were all created by Kipling, and where politics is kept at arm's length. The historical fantasies in *Puck of Pook's Hill* and *Rewards and Fairies* have their strengths as well, and the three volumes taken together are powerful examples of Kipling's contribution to fantasy as a genre. It is worth acknowledging, though, that the later volumes are timebound by Edwardian anxieties. Like Toad Hall in Kenneth Grahame's *The Wind in the Willows* (1908), the setting of Parnesius in these stories is an embattled place, threatened by change. For 'Roman Empire' read 'British Empire': the unravelling of the former reflects Kipling's anxieties about England's unreadiness to defend its position in the world. He aired his fears most famously in his 1902 poem, 'The Islanders', where England's officer class have become 'the flannelled fools at the wicket or the muddied oafs at the goal'. Kipling's Roman stories in *Puck of Pook's Hill* and his English historical stories in *Rewards and Fairies* show where he was coming from.

The Beginning of the Armadilloes

The poem 'Farewell, Rewards and Fairies' by Richard Corbett, Bishop of Oxford, and subsequently of Norwich (1582–1635), was itself a playful elegy for another lost empire, that of the Church of Rome.

> Farewell, rewards and *Faeries*,
> Good Housewives now may say;
> For now foul Slutts in dairies
> Do fare as well as they.

The poem is earthy and witty, acknowledging the laxity of the old system while mourning its loss:

> Lament, lament, old Abbies,
> The *Faeries* lost Command:
> They did but change Priests *Babies*,
> But some have changed your *Land*.[19]

The beauty and mystery of Roman Catholic England have given way to a greyer and sterner regime. Corbett was a genial, broadminded and generous-spirited priest. His playfully detached perspective on the troubles of his time finds a happy equivalence in the imaginative freedom of Kipling's *Just so Stories*.

8

HOW THE FIRST LETTER WAS WRITTEN

Once upon a most early time was a Neolithic man. He was not a Jute or an Angle, or even a Dravidian, which he might well have been, Best Beloved, but never mind why. He was a Primitive, and he lived cavily in a Cave, and he wore very few clothes, and he couldn't read and he couldn't write and he didn't want to, and except when he was hungry he was quite happy. His name was Tegumai Bopsulai, and that means, 'Man-who-does-not-put-his-foot-forward-in-a-hurry'; but we, O Best Beloved, will call him Tegumai, for short. And his wife's name was Teshumai Tewindrow, that means, 'Lady-who-asks-a-very-many-questions'; but we, O Best Beloved, will call her Teshumai, for short. And his little girl-daughter's name was Taffimai Metallumai, and that means, 'Small-person-without-any-manners-who-ought-to-be-spanked'; but I'm going to call her Taffy. And she was Tegumai Bopsulai's Best Beloved and her own Mummy's Best Beloved, and she was not spanked half as much as was good for her; and they were all three very happy.[1]

Carrie Kipling's diary[2] for 19 September 1900 refers to this story as 'Neolithic Ladies'. The Neolithic family living 'cavily in a Cave' recalls the pioneering spirit with which Kipling and Carrie first settled in Vermont, living in the rugged discomfort of Bliss Cottage. But 'Taffimai' herself in this story is based on their daughter Josephine when she had reached the age of 6, which was after the Kipling family had returned to

England. By this date they had rented the ill-omened Rock House near Torquay.*

> Now attend and listen! One day Tegumai Bopsulai went down through the beaver-swamp to the Wagai river to spear carp-fish for dinner, and Taffy went too. Tegumai's spear was made of wood with shark's teeth at the end, and before he had caught any fish at all he accidentally broke it clean across by jabbing it down too hard on the bottom of the river. They were miles and miles from home (of course they had their lunch with them in a little bag), and Tegumai had forgotten to bring any extra spears.[3]

Taffimai offers to run back to the Cave for a second spear, but Tegumai protests that the distance is too far and the path is dangerous. Taffimai then comes up with a revolutionary thought (which the adult reader, looking over the child's shoulder, will recognise as one which embodies a step-change in human development): 'I say, Daddy, it's an awful nuisance that you and I don't know how to write, isn't it? If we did we could send a message for the new spear.' Tegumai then detains (and entertains) us with a complete side-issue ('how often have I told you not to use slang? "Awful" isn't a pretty word') before he is willing to acknowledge that his daughter is right.[4]

A 'Stranger-man' from another tribe, a 'Tewara', is accosted by Taffimai. The consequent comic misunderstanding underscores Neolithic man's need for written communication. Taffimai attempts to communicate with him in two stages, first in sign language and then by making a drawing. 'First I'll draw Daddy fishing,' and then 'I'll draw the other spear that he wants.' She adds 'a picture of me myself 'splaining to you', and

---

* See my discussion of the haunted house in Kipling's story 'The House Surgeon' in chapter 1.

'Now I'll draw you.' She apologises for her picture of him: 'I can't make you pretty in the picture, so you mustn't be 'fended. Are you 'fended?' Her drawing becomes more elaborate and is in effect a map, giving a route past some trees, over a hill and across a beaver-swamp to Tegumai's Cave.[5] The hapless Tewara man is mystified by Taffimai's drawing, and his interpretation of it is ingenious but wholly wrong: 'If I do not fetch this great Chief's tribe to help him, he will be slain by his enemies who are coming up on all sides with spears.' There must be 'a big battle going to be fought somewhere' and the 'extraordinary child' Taffimai is 'telling me to call the great Chief's tribe to help him.'[6]

A running joke in the text emphasises the strangeness of the friendly Tewara by making his distinctive tribal name part of a pattern. This sets up a pleasing nonsensical structure of which the word 'Tewara' provides the basic building block. The Stranger-man 'came along the river, but he belonged to a far tribe, the Tewaras, and he did not understand one word of Tegumai's language'. The little group becomes locked in a thicket of friendly and polite misunderstanding (of the kind that overtakes middle-class English holidaymakers seeking to make themselves understood in, say, Croatia). The repetition of 'Tewara' underscores the divide: 'The Stranger-man (*and* he was a Tewara) thought, "This is a very, very wonderful child. She waves her arms and she shouts at me, but I don't understand a word of what she says."' This pattern's relentlessness develops into a secondary cumulative joke: 'The Stranger-man (and *he* was a Tewara)', 'The Stranger-man (and he *was* a Tewara)', 'The Stranger-man (and he was *a* Tewara)', 'The Stranger-man (and he was a *Tewara*)'.

Taffimai takes the Tewara's shark's tooth. 'The Stranger-man (and he *was* a Tewara) thought, "This is a very, very, very wonderful child. The shark's tooth on my necklace is a magic shark's tooth, and I was always told that if anybody touched it without my leave they would immediately swell up or burst."'[7] Overawed by what he takes to be Taffimai's occult powers, he surrenders his shark's tooth, and with it she scratches into a

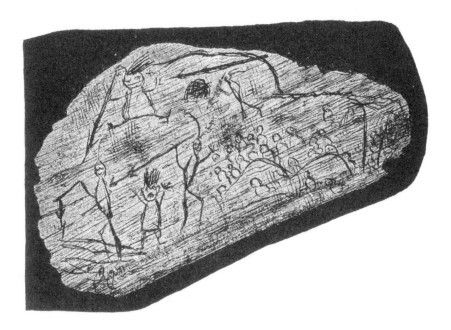

piece of birch-bark a picture narrative of what has happened to Tegumai, and of what she wants the Tewara to do (to find his way to her parental Cave and bring her father's spear).[8] The story then develops into an extended joke about the perils of misreading. The Tewara takes the drawing as a warning of war between the tribes.* Having decided that he understands Taffimai's drawing, the Tewara 'raced off into the bushes like the wind, with the birch-bark in his hand'. The Tewara man finds the cave of Taffimai's parents. At this point the story has become decidedly pleased with its own jovial tone:

---

* In Kipling's mind, narratives of tribal warfare at this date were likely to have reflected the current hostilities between the European 'tribes' in southern Africa, the British settlers and the two Dutch republics, the Transvaal and the Orange Free State; the conflict in which, as we have seen, Kipling was fiercely committed to the British cause and especially to the ambitions of his friend Cecil Rhodes.

The Stranger-man – did you know he was a Tewara? – hurried away with the picture and ran for some miles, till quite by accident he found Teshumai Tewindrow at the door of her Cave, talking to some other Neolithic ladies who had come in to a Primitive lunch. Taffy was very like Teshumai, specially about the upper part of the face and the eyes, so the Stranger-man – always a pure Tewara – smiled politely and handed Teshumai the birch-bark. He had run hard, so that he panted, and his legs were scratched with brambles, but he still tried to be polite.

His courteous approach to Teshumai and her friends precipitates a scene of knockabout farce: 'As soon as Teshumai saw the picture she screamed like anything and flew at the Stranger-man. The other Neolithic ladies at once knocked him down and sat on him in a long line of six, while Teshumai pulled his hair.' Teshumai's reading of Taffimai's picture is that it is evidence of murder:

'Here is my Tegumai with his arm broken; here is a spear sticking into his back; here is a man with a spear ready to throw; here is another man throwing a spear from a Cave, and here are a whole pack of people' (they were Taffy's beavers, really, but they did look rather like people) 'coming up behind Tegumai. Isn't it shocking!' 'Most shocking!' said the Neolithic ladies, and they filled the Stranger-man's hair with mud.[9]

The Tewara endures their insults and assaults while the tribe of Tegumai is summoned, and then leads them back to the riverbank where Taffy and Tegumai are waiting. 'It has ruined all my fishing for the day' is Tegumai's reasonable reaction to the presence of his 'whole dear, kind, nice, clean, quiet Tribe'. The ironic tone reminds us of the Elephant's Child going home to 'all his dear families' in order to spank them with his trunk. Kipling's listing of the tribe fills a whole paragraph, closing with 'feudal and prognathous Villeins, semi-entitled to half a bearskin of winter nights, seven yards from the fire, and adscript serfs, holding the reversion of a scraped marrow-bone under heriot (Aren't those beautiful words, Best Beloved?).'

Taffy sees her friendly 'Stranger-man' being ill-treated by the Neolithic ladies and intervenes: 'What are you doing to my nice Stranger-man?' The misunderstanding is both tribal and matrimonial. There is no meeting of minds between Tegumai and his wife:

'Where are the bad people who speared you, my darling?' said Teshumai Tewindrow. 'There weren't any,' said Tegumai. 'My only visitor this morning was the poor fellow that you are trying to choke. Aren't you well, or are you ill, O Tribe of Tegumai?'

It then becomes clear to Tegumai and Taffy (who 'did not feel quite comfy') that Taffy's drawing has been the source of the ill-treatment of the Tewara, and she explains slowly and carefully what the intentions were behind her drawing. She finishes by turning on her own tribe with commendable spirit:

'*I* think you are just the stupidest people in the world,' said Taffy. 'He is a very nice man. Why have you filled his hair with mud? Wash him!'

Nobody said anything at all for a long time, till the Head Chief laughed; then the Stranger-man (who was at least a Tewara) laughed; then Tegumai laughed till he fell down flat on the bank; then all the Tribe laughed more and worse and louder. The only people who did not laugh were Teshumai Tewindrow and the Neolithic ladies. They were very polite to their husbands, and said 'idiot!' ever so often.[10]

Festive comedy, from *A Winter's Tale* to *The Importance of Being Earnest*, typically closes with a celebration of inclusion. The Tewara is adopted into the Tribe of Tegumai, the Head Chief predicts that what Taffy has devised will lead to the twenty-six letters of the alphabet, and the story resolves itself with harmony. Nobody is left out.

Did Kipling need to resort to such broad farce for the purposes of this story? He enjoyed farce, and had created some other skilful and carefully constructed tales based on misunderstanding of the type found here. Examples of these are 'My Sunday at Home' and 'Brugglesmith', collected in 1898 and 1899 respectively. 'My Sunday at Home' (written in 1894) is set in Wiltshire and was completed at Tisbury, where Kipling's parents had retired when Lockwood Kipling had finished his work in India. It turns on misunderstanding: an American doctor visiting England volunteers to treat an 'enormous navvy' whom he believes to have taken laudanum. In fact the navvy is simply very drunk; the doctor medicates him with an emetic and the navvy then vomits copiously and blames the doctor for his physical misery, and refuses to let go of him. The doctor's expensive coat needs to be cut open before he can escape. The joke again turns on drink in 'Brugglesmith'. Here the narrator is a newly famous young writer (Kipling himself, lightly disguised) who finds himself cornered by a series of farcical events into accompanying a drunken Scot back to his home, Brugglesmith (a slurred drunk's version of 'Brook Green, Hammersmith'). This tale is little more than an extended shaggy-dog story, deliberately far too long for the tiny germ of its plot.

The laughter in these second-division farces is male. During his blighted childhood years in Southsea Kipling had the release and refreshment of annual Christmas visits to his 'Aunt Georgy', Georgiana Burne-Jones, at The Grange in Kensington. The Grange (now demolished) stood at the Kensington end of North End Road, and had belonged earlier to the eighteenth-century novelist Samuel Richardson, author of the epistolary novels *Pamela* (1740–1) and *Sir Charles Grandison* (1754). Kipling remembered the extraordinary delight of staying in this house as a child, recalling in particular the evenings when he and his Burne-Jones cousins heard the voices of the adult world below. 'We could hang over the stairs and listen to the loveliest sound in the world – deep-voiced men laughing together over dinner.'[11] This was resurrected in his autobiography

nearly seventy years later. It takes adjustment to acknowledge that
'Brugglesmith' and the over-farcical story about the Tewara and the
Neolithic ladies come from the same writer who created such perfectly
balanced narratives as 'The Elephant's Child' and 'How the Leopard got his
Spots'. 'How the First Letter was Written' comes from a breezier part of
Kipling's mind, experience and method.

The insistence on drawing as a form of communication points up the
significance of Kipling's own drawings in this tale. The O of 'Once upon
a time' gives another instance of Noah's Ark.[12] This Ark is painted with
Plimsoll lines (the line showing the point above which a vessel is
overloaded) and its flag bears the letters N, H, S and J (the initials of
Noah, Ham, Shem and Japheth). The extreme antiquity of the Ark is
reflected in the extreme antiquity of Tegumai himself, the primitive who
wore very few clothes.

The story of 'The First Letter' marks a decisive change of direction in
the *Just so Stories* in that, here, humans, not talking animals, take centre
stage. The ladies as a group create the main action of the story's farcical
climax as they attack the polite Tewara man, after which the whole tribe
together with Tegumai's family find resolution in laughter. The Head Chief

sees the point of Taffy's device: 'O Small-person-without-any-manners-who-ought-to-be-spanked, you've hit upon a great invention!'[13] The caption to this image tells us: 'this is the story of Taffimai Metallumai carved on an old tusk a very long time ago by the Ancient Peoples'. It is written in 'runes' of Kipling's invention. From top left the first sentence of the script reads: 'This is the stori of Taffimai all ritten out on an old tusk.' The equivalent sentence top right reads: 'The reason that I spell it queerly is because there are not enugh letters in the Runic alphabet for all the ourds that I ouant to use to u o Belofed.'*[14] The game Kipling played here with the Runic alphabet was consistent with the constant detailed focus on the craft of writing, linked to his pleasure in technical innovation, which shows in some of his most ingenious stories.

Writing is in its infancy in the Taffimai story, and wireless telegraphy is in its infancy in a story from the same phase of Kipling's writing life as the publication of the *Just so Stories*. This is reflected in the supernatural story 'Wireless', collected in *Traffics & Discoveries* in 1904. Here a chemist's assistant (named 'Shaynor') falls into a trance-like state and writes out fragments of Keats' 'The Eve of St Agnes' and 'Ode to a Nightingale', transmitted through him as though by radio waves from Keats' long-dead spirit. (Shaynor coughs blood into his handkerchief and is clearly suffering from tuberculosis, the disease which killed Keats.) At the same time the chemist's nephew is operating a wireless set with which he seeks to pick up radio messages coming from Poole harbour ('a charged wire at Poole, giving out these waves into space'). They experience 'something coming through from somewhere; but it isn't Poole', while the astonished narrator watches this otherwise unremarkable young man channelling Keats' spirit.

Kipling had recently met Guglielmo Marconi, who had since 1895 been developing wireless telegraphy as a revolutionary mode of communication. Psychic communication and Marconi's invention were united in this tale.[15] In the hands of contemporary writers experimenting with the supernatural – Arthur Machen, Algernon Blackwood or M.R. James, for example – the channelling of Keats' spirit could have been clunky and over-sensationalised, whereas Kipling's handling of it is spare, economical and quiet in tone. The fact that the spirit of Keats is dictating 'The Eve of St Agnes' to a man who has never read the poem (and does not recognise Keats' name) is introduced slowly, building up from individual words. ' "Manna – manna – manna", he said at last, under wrinkled brows':

---

* In the comic-strip illustrations carved on the piece of tusk the figure of Teshumai Tewindrow, Taffimai's mother, is clearly an affectionate caricature of Carrie Kipling.

'That's what I wanted. Good! Now then! Now then!' [...] His voice rose and he spoke rightly and fully without a falter: –

Candied apple, quince and plum and gourd,
And jellies smoother than the creamy curd,
And lucent syrups tinct with cinnamon,
Manna and dates in Argosy transferred
From Fez; and spiced dainties, every one
From silken Samarcand to cedared Lebanon.

After a moment's faltering he corrects 'smoother' to 'soother'. 'It came away under his hand as it is written in the book – as it is written in the book.'[16] The narrator's stunned repetition of this phrase brings home the impossible wonder of what is happening here.

An earlier story, 'The Finest Story in the World' (collected in *Many Inventions*), has a similar fantasy base. Charlie Mears, a city bank clerk who aspires to be a writer but is devoid of talent, is the channel for the narratives of both a Greek galley-slave and a Viking sailor. He wants to offer an idea that he has, 'the story of a ship', as material for the narrator, an established writer, to use. Charlie's material is astonishingly specific and it is clear to the reader, if not immediately to the narrator, that Charlie's account of the ships in which he has served are transmitted to him from the remote past. The central figure of Charlie's Greek galley story is a former pirate, now a slave chained to his oar:

With an iron band round his waist fixed to the bench he sits on, and a sort of handcuff on his left wrist chaining him to the oar. He's on the lower deck where the worst men are sent, and the only light comes from the hatchways and through the oar-holes. [...] When a man dies at his oar on that deck he isn't thrown overboard, but cut up in his chains and stuffed through the oar-hole in little pieces.[17]

Charlie writes part of his story in Ancient Greek, a language of which he has no knowledge (it needs to be translated for the narrator by an expert at the British Museum). The narrator is in possession of 'the most marvellous tale in the world, nothing less than the story of a Greek galley-slave, as told by himself'.[18]

Charlie's memories hold a further surprise: he has had a series of further incarnations, and in particular recalls (as a free man) joining a Viking hero in the ninth or tenth century. 'He came from the north; they said so in the galley when he looked for rowers – not slaves, but free men.' In this incarnation Charlie has rowed to 'Wineland', in North America: 'Was it possible that he had skipped half a dozen lives, and was then dimly remembering some episode of a thousand years later?'[19] The story closes bathetically. Charlie's unique gift is destroyed by his sex drive. He becomes passionately involved with a young woman – his first such experience – and his memories of his previous lives are all immediately lost to him. The miraculous flow has gone.*

'The Finest Story in the World' and 'Wireless' were published at either end of the decade in which Kipling wrote his *Just so Stories*, and may be taken as additional reflections on the activity of writing explored in the Taffimai stories. In these stories the writer is in the possession of a force, and Kipling's name for the force in his own case was his Daemon. In *Something of Myself* he declared his faith in it: 'When your Daemon is in charge, do not try to think consciously. Drift, wait, and obey.'[20] A very late tale about the craft of writing, 'Proofs of Holy Writ', clearly displays Kipling's faith in his own writerly Daemon. In this story, Shakespeare and Ben Jonson have met in the garden of Shakespeare's house near Stratford in about 1611. Both of them are charged with the duty of assisting the

---

* Does this echo a fear from Kipling's earlier years that his creative energy would be curtailed by marriage? Kipling wrote a complete draft of a novel called *Mother Maturin* which is known to have dealt explicitly with the seamier aspects of Indian life. The manuscript has vanished; it is possible that Carrie found its content tasteless and exercised censorship.

team of learned clerics who are creating the translation of the Bible now known as the King James Bible, and are at work on the text of Isaiah 60:1–3 and 19. Jonson is scholarly and systematic while Shakespeare trusts to his instincts and comes up with phrases for the translation which may be approximate but are nevertheless far more expressive than Jonson's offerings. Shakespeare is possessed by a force. 'Proofs of Holy Writ' creates a kind of dynastic succession in which inspiration from the biblical text pours into Kipling's mind and thence into his characterisation of Shakespeare. Kipling's Shakespeare creates the first verses of Isaiah 60 in a form which is close to the King James Bible as we have it: 'Rise – shine; for thy light is come, and the glory of the Lord is risen on thee. For, behold, darkness shall cloke the earth, and gross darkness the people. But the Lord shall arise on thee, and His glory shall be seen upon thee.' (King James here reads: 'Arise, shine; for thy light is come, and the glory of the Lord is risen upon thee. For, behold, the darkness shall cover the earth, and gross darkness the people: but the Lord shall arise upon thee, and his glory shall be seen upon thee.') Shakespeare speaks directly for Kipling here: 'My Demon never betrayed me yet, while I trusted him.' While translating Isaiah 60:20 he is physically possessed: 'He began to thump Ben on the shoulder.' 'We have it!' His translation ends: 'The sun shall no more go down; neither shall thy moon withdraw herself, for the Lord shall be thine everlasting light, and the days of thy mourning shall be ended.'[21]

In the 'Working-Tools' chapter of *Something of Myself*, Kipling wrote that 'the mere act of writing was, and always has been, a physical pleasure to me', with the consequence that he was happy to cut and discard. He makes an analogy with a pianist. It was 'easier to throw away any thing that did not turn out well: and to practise, as it were, scales'.[22] Kipling wrote when thinking about the start of his work on the 'Anglo-Indian tales' (by which he meant his *Plain Tales from the Hills*) that they:

> were originally much longer than when they appeared, but the shortening of them, first to my own fancy after rapturous re-readings,

and next to the space available, taught me that a tale from which pieces have been raked out is like a fire that has been poked. One does not know that the operation has been performed, but everyone feels the effect.

To the metaphor of raking out the pieces Kipling added the notion of letting his writing 'drain'. This also is a creative action, but of a different kind from 'raking'. 'Read your final draft,' he advises:

and consider faithfully every paragraph, sentence and word, blacking out where requisite. Let it lie by to drain as long as possible. At the end of that time, re-read and you should find that it will bear a second shortening. Finally, read it aloud alone and at leisure. Maybe a shade more brushwork will then indicate or impose itself. [. . .] If not, praise Allah and let it go, and 'when thou has done, repent not.'

He added that 'I have had tales by me for three or five years which shortened themselves almost yearly. The magic lies in the Brush and the Ink.'[23]

'Raking out', 'draining' and 'brushwork' are three different procedures, and all three metaphors invite us to look at the *Just so Stories* as carefully worked pieces in which the illustrations (all in black and white, with the exception of the red for the explorer's route up the Amazon shown in the Armadillo tale) complement and supplement the dramatic content of the narrative. Kipling's art in these stories displays a composite of skills, visual and verbal, poetry as well as prose. A sketch by Lockwood Kipling of about 1880 uses comic hyperbole to make grand claims for his clever son. It is what Kipling called a 'scandalous sepia-sketch of Tennyson and Browning in procession, and a spectacled school-boy bringing up the rear.'[24] 'Scandalous' is more than mock modesty: Kipling shared Lockwood's high estimation of his own talent and promise, and the notion that he belonged to the same league as Tennyson and Browning was not aired wholly in jest.

Kipling owed much to Browning and less to Tennyson. These two Victorians both became socially grand in their respective ways (Tennyson markedly so). Tennyson's wife, Emily, committed herself wholeheartedly to her husband's upward social mobility, and when he was offered a baronetcy by Gladstone it was Emily who told him to reject it and to hold out for the grander title of Baron Tennyson. Kipling, by contrast, had no such ambitions. With any gathering of men his impulse was to immerse himself in the group rather than to transcend it. He deeply loved the sense of being an insider, be it with soldiers, the British in Simla, the Indians whose intimacy served him so well when he wrote *Kim* or the engineers and technicians whose expertise he envied and wanted to understand; in all such groups he wanted to know, from within, the nature of other men's lives and work, and to be accepted as one of them.

9

HOW THE ALPHABET WAS MADE

The week after Taffimai Metallumai (we will still call her Taffy, Best Beloved) made that little mistake about her Daddy's spear and the Stranger-man and the picture-letter and all, she went carp-fishing again with her Daddy. Her Mummy wanted her to stay at home and help hang up hides to dry on the big drying-poles outside their Neolithic Cave, but Taffy slipped away down to her Daddy quite early, and they fished. Presently she began to giggle, and her Daddy said 'Don't be silly, child.'

'But wasn't it inciting!' said Taffy. 'Don't you remember how the Head Chief puffed out his cheeks, and how funny the nice Stranger-man looked with the mud in his hair?' 'Well do I,' said Tegumai. 'I had to pay two deerskins – soft ones with fringes – to the Stranger-man for the things we did to him.'

'*We* didn't do anything,' said Taffy. 'It was Mummy and the other Neolithic ladies – and the mud.'

'We won't talk about that,' said her Daddy. 'Let's have lunch.'

Taffy took a marrow-bone and sat mousy-quiet for ten whole minutes, while her Daddy scratched on pieces of birch-bark with a shark's tooth. Then she said, 'Daddy, I've thinked of a secret surprise. You make a noise – any sort of noise.'

'Ah!' said Tegumai. 'Will that do to begin with?'

'Yes,' said Taffy. 'You look just like a carp-fish with its mouth open. Say it again, please.'

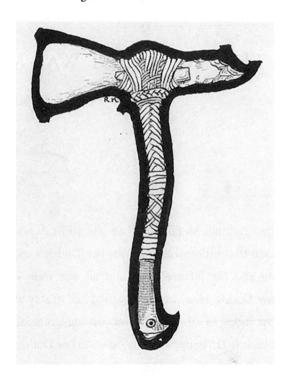

'Ah! ah! ah!' said her Daddy. 'Don't be rude, my daughter.'

'I'm not meaning rude, really and truly,' said Taffy. 'It's part of my secret-surprise-think. *Do* say *ah*, Daddy, and keep your mouth open at the end, and lend me that tooth. I'm going to draw a carp-fish's mouth wide-open.'[1]

Taffy makes her drawing, and the carp's mouth becomes the letter A.[2]

The laughter in 'How the First Letter was Written' did not conclude the story's plot, such as it was – the basis of the misunderstanding was not solved – and the point at which the misunderstanding was explained to the tribe of Tegumai and Taffimai called for the origin of writing to be explored. 'How the Alphabet was Made' assumes knowledge of 'How the First Letter was Written'. (Linking two narratives in this way was a departure from the method of the seven previous stories, each of which could stand on its own.) 'How the Alphabet was Made' invents ways in which Neolithic

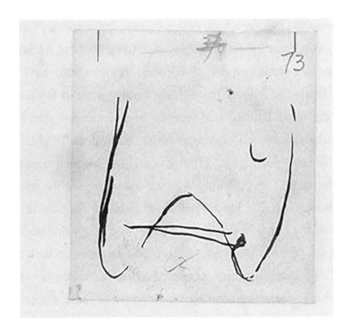

man could have turned pictures into letters. The 'a' or 'ah' sound is represented by 'a carp-fish with its mouth open', and further sounds are represented by the carp's tail, by an egg, and so forth. The Tegumai word for water is YA and the word for bad water is YO. Kipling's drawings have illustrated Y as a carp-tail and O as an egg so that Taffy can confidently say: 'Carp-tail and round egg. Two noises mixed! *Yo*, bad water.'[3]

Kipling enjoyed his own ingenuity in these images. The best of his illustrations for this story is the elaborate image of 'a magic Alphabet-necklace of all the letters', in which he places a family joke in the form of a hidden tribute to his father. 'J is a fish-hook in mother-of-pearl. L is the broken spear in silver. (K ought to follow J, of course, but the necklace was broken once and they mended it wrong.) K is a thin slice of bone scratched and rubbed in black.'[4] It would have required an adult to explain to the child audience that the real reason for changing JKL to the sequence 'JLK' is that JLK stands for their grandfather, John Lockwood Kipling.

Following the death of Tennyson in 1892 Kipling had become the uncrowned Poet Laureate. The official post of Laureate was left vacant for four years until 1896, by which date a Conservative victory had brought in Lord Salisbury as Prime Minister. Salisbury's nephew, Arthur Balfour, pressed for the appointment of Kipling. There would have been no objection from the Palace. The Kipling family were in favour with the Queen (Lockwood Kipling had recently been commissioned to create a suite of Indian rooms at Osborne House on the Isle of Wight). Salisbury could see the case for Kipling ('though he blows his own trumpet rather loud sometimes'),[5] but Kipling himself maintained his resistance to public honours of this kind. 'A discreet inquiry quickly revealed his antipathy to any official recognition', and consequently Balfour's proposal was dropped. In what looks like a gesture of impatience with the whole business Lord Salisbury then appointed Alfred Austen, a versifying civil servant whose work had nothing to commend it, and whose tenure of the Laureateship would come to be regarded with universal contempt.[6]

The draw of The Elms at Rottingdean, which Kipling rented from 1897 to 1902, was that his beloved uncle Sir Edward Burne-Jones was often staying in his house there for summer breaks. In 1898 this comfortable situation was destabilised: 'Uncle Ned' died suddenly on 17 June. Kipling wrote to his American friend Charles Eliot Norton that Burne-Jones had been 'more to me than any man here: over and above my own life's love for him: and he had changed my life in many ways'. He was an example and a fellow craftsman: 'The man was a God to me – as a workman I can't tell you about *that* side of it and it doesn't very much matter now.'[7]

A second family disaster came later in the year. His beautiful and gifted sister Alice ('Trix') had stayed in India for many years in support of her husband's career, but in the autumn she and her husband came home. The family had known for some years that she had fragile mental health, and in December 1898 her problems reached a point where she had to be looked after by Alice Kipling, her and Rudyard's mother.[8] Kipling turned increasingly for security to Carrie and his own three children.

In the winter of that year the Kiplings took an abrupt decision to sail to New York. Carrie wanted to see her mother; and Kipling had his own reasons for needing to cross the Atlantic again. He was caught up in a vexatious dispute over the copyright to his works which were being published without his authority in the United States. The Kiplings sailed from Liverpool and had the roughest crossing they had ever experienced; the whole family were weakened by seasickness and the three children, together with the nurse appointed to look after them, became ill. Things did not improve after they docked in New York on 2 February 1899. Carrie also became ill, and although she recovered quite well this was not the case for the three children, who could not throw off their infections. They stayed in a hotel, never an ideal setting for a serious illness. Kipling himself became ill, and friends rallied round them, especially their long-established American physician friend, Dr Conland, from Brattleboro, though he brought additional anxiety. He reported that Beatty Balestier was coming to New York in order to sue Kipling for $50,000 'on a charge of malicious prosecution' (when Kipling had taken Beatty to court three years previously, in 1896).[9]

Kipling and his daughter Josephine both developed pneumonia. For several weeks Kipling's life was thought to be in danger, and Carrie decided to move Josephine from the hotel to the home of some friends on Long Island. This was 22 February 1899, still in bad weather, and Josephine had a very high temperature. Moving a sick child in these circumstances was obviously not ideal, but Carrie was doing her best. In the last week of February the doctors were warning that Kipling was likely to die. He was by now the most celebrated of all English writers, and still only 32 years old. His illness had become world news, and fresh bulletins about him were published each day. By 1 March he showed signs of recovery and by 4 March he had turned a corner; but two days later, on 6 March, his daughter Josephine died. Carrie displayed iron self-control, and kept knowledge of Josephine's death from Kipling for over two weeks. On the day of Josephine's interment Kipling was delirious.

Dressed in black, Carrie went straight from her daughter's funeral to Kipling's bedside and had to borrow a red scarf at the last moment in order to disguise the fact that she was in mourning for their daughter. Kipling was not to know.[10]

Each of the two Taffimai stories is followed by verse. Grief for Josephine had been held back by laughter in the main narrative of 'How

Formal portrait of Josephine

Josephine in the garden of Naulakha

the First Letter was Written', and by gentle admiration for the child's cleverness in the text of 'How the Alphabet was Made', but it returns in full force in the stanzas about Merrow Down which conclude the two stories. (Merrow Down is near Guildford, in Surrey, and was at that time a village where Kipling often visited his friend St Loe Strachey. Other place names in the poem are also in Surrey: Bramley, Shere, Shamley Green and the River Wey.) The stanzas comprise a single poem split into two halves. It is in the second half, closing 'How the Alphabet was Made', that Kipling's grief for Josephine is fully felt.

The first part of the poem imagines a track leading out of the village where 'the ancient Britons dressed and rode/ To watch the dark Phoenicians bring/ Their goods along the Western Road', and then recedes into prehistory:

But long and long before that time
(When bison used to roam on it)
Did Taffy and her Daddy climb
That down, and had their home on it.

It closes: 'All the Tribe of Tegumai/ They cut a noble figure then!' At the
end of 'How the Alphabet was Made' the poem about Merrow Down
resumes:

Of all the Tribe of Tegumai
Who cut that figure, none remain, –
On Merrow Down the cuckoos cry –
The silence and the sun remain.

But as the faithful years return
And hearts unwounded sing again,
Comes Taffy dancing through the fern
To lead the Surrey spring again.

Her brows are bound with bracken-fronds,
And golden elf-locks fly above;
Her eyes are bright as diamonds
And bluer than the skies above.

In moccasins and deer-skin cloak,
Unfearing, free and fair she flits,
And lights her little damp-wood smoke
To show her Daddy where she flits.

For far – oh, very far behind,
So far she cannot call to him,
Comes Tegumai alone to find
The daughter that was all to him.[11]

How the Alphabet was Made

There are other writings in which Kipling dwelt on this bereavement, especially the supernatural story called 'They', published in *Scribner's Magazine* and then collected in *Traffics and Discoveries*. 'They' is one of Kipling's most carefully structured and paced stories of the supernatural. A motorist in Sussex drives delightedly and aimlessly through the countryside, as was Kipling's habit when he first settled in Sussex. The landscape instructs the motorist in its history:

> I found hidden villages where bees, the only things awake, boomed in eighty-foot lindens that overhung grey Norman churches; miraculous brooks diving under stone bridges built for heavier traffic than would ever vex them again; tithe-barns larger than their churches, and an old smithy that cried out aloud how it had once been a hall of the Knights of the Temple.

He takes a wrong turning and drives his car into the grounds of a private house:

> An ancient house of lichened and weather-worn stone, with mullioned windows and roofs of rose-red tile. It was flanked by semi-circular walls, also rose-red, that closed the lawn on the fourth side, and at their feet a box hedge grew man-high. There were doves on the roof about the slim brick chimneys, and I caught a glimpse of an octagonal dove-house behind the screening wall.[12]

At the heart of this luxurious setting is a direct link with Kipling's personal tragedy, which he projects into the experience of his lightly disguised fictional motorist. The Elizabethan house is lived in by a blind woman surrounded by children to whom she devotes her life. The motorist visits the house a number of times, driving from what the blind woman speaks of as 'the other side of the county' (the phrase hints that he has driven from the country of the living to that of the dead). He gradually learns that the children are ghosts, and that because his own child, a daughter, has died, he is privileged to see them.

T.S. Eliot was attracted by the central motif of the story – dead children haunting a lovely setting – and used it in the earliest of his *Four Quartets* (he was writing the poem in the last year of Kipling's life, and it was first published in 1936). Kipling's ghostly children appear in the garden of the house near Chipping Camden, Burnt Norton, in which Eliot set his poem of the same name.[13]

The central revelation in Kipling's story is understated, and all the more effective for its emotional restraint. The narrator sits to observe the blind lady dealing with one of her tenants, a grasping farmer who is trying to cheat her, and who is frightened by the house (presumably because he senses that it is haunted): 'His eyes rolled into every corner of the room wide with horror.' Kipling adds a landowner's aside about the farmer's conflicted impulses: 'I could not but admire the intensity of his greed, when I saw him out-facing for its sake whatever terror it was that ran wet on his forehead.' Immediately following this comes the revelation for the narrator himself:

> The little brushing kiss fell in the centre of my palm – as a gift on which the fingers were, once, expected to close: as the all-faithful half-reproachful signal of a waiting child not used to neglect even when the grown-ups were busiest – a fragment of the mute code devised very long ago.
>
> Then I knew. And it was as though I had known from the first day when I looked across the lawn at the high window.

The intensity of his feeling at the moment of recognition that this is his own dead child is well controlled, as is the suffering he undergoes in the subsequent dialogue. The ghosts come to their bereaved parents. The blind woman has had no children of her own, and the children began coming to her house led by the dead child of her butler's wife.

The blind woman regrets that she has 'neither borne nor lost!' and the narrator's response, again, feels like a bravely exposed expression of Kipling's own pain:

> 'Be very glad then,' said I, for my soul was torn open within me.
>> 'Forgive me!'
>
> She was still, and I went back to my sorrow and my joy.[14]

10

THE CRAB THAT PLAYED
WITH THE SEA

Before the High and Far-Off Times, O my Best Beloved, came the
time of the Very Beginnings; and that was in the days when the Eldest
Magician was getting Things ready. First he got the Earth ready; then
he got the Sea ready; and then he told all the Animals that they could
come out and play. And the Animals said, 'O Eldest Magician, what
shall we play at?' and he said, 'I will show you.' He took the Elephant
– All-the-Elephant-there-was – and said, 'Play at being an Elephant,'
and All-the-Elephant-there-was played. He took the Beaver – All-the-
Beaver-there-was – and said 'Play at being a Beaver,' and All-the-
Beaver-there-was played. He took the Cow – All-the-Cow-there-was
– and said, 'Play at being a Cow,' and All-the-Cow-there-was played.
He took the Turtle – All-the-Turtle-there-was – and said, 'Play at
being a Turtle,' and All-the-Turtle-there-was played. One by one he
took all the beasts and birds and fishes and told them what to play at.[1]

In the winter of 1901 Kipling finished 'The Crab that Played with the Sea'
and then set out with Carrie for his annual winter holiday in the Cape.
There he wrote 'The Cat that Walked by Himself' and 'The Butterfly that
Stamped' in the first few months of 1902. In 'The Crab that Played with
the Sea' Kipling points us to the moment *before* the primal act of creation
('Before the High and Far-Off Times') and catches the Eldest Magician in
the act of creating the known universe and our present world. His
sentences affectionately shadow and echo Genesis and also embrace the

myth of creation as set out in the Quran; Adam and his progeny, and the story of Noah's Flood, appear in both the Arabic and the Jewish texts. Kipling's story gives in miniature a composite of most of the creation myths of the early religions, Christian, Islamic, Hindu and Buddhist. The tone of Kipling's narrative is redolent with open wonder in the face of a supernatural event, and simultaneously interpolates in a touching aside the author's own relationship with his eldest child:

> Towards evening, when people and things grow restless and tired, there came up the Man (With his own little girl-daughter?) – Yes, with his own best-beloved little girl-daughter sitting upon his shoulder, and he said, 'What is this play, Eldest Magician?' And the Eldest Magician said, 'Ho, son of Adam, this is the play of the Very Beginning; but you are too wise for this play.' And the man saluted and said, 'Yes, I am too wise for this play; but see that you make all the Animals obedient to me.'[2]

The first plate is rich in significance. The caption tells us that it is 'Big Medicine and Strong Magic'. The man is in conversation with the Magician, who holds three lotus flowers (the lotus is associated with the birth of the central figure in Buddhist, Egyptian and Hindu traditions). All-the-Elephant-there-was, All-the-Cow-there-was and All-the-Turtle-there-was are leaving the scene by going over the crest of the hill at the top of the image, and the other animals are fulfilling the Magician's instructions to be themselves and to play on this side of the hill (Tiger, Elk, Parrot, Monkey and Snake, as well as All-the-Bunnies-there-were).[3] The hump in the centre of the water is Pau Amma the Crab, hiding himself from the Eldest Magician.

Pau Amma is hiding because he has chosen to be disobedient: he 'scuttled off sideways and stepped into the sea, saying to himself, "I will play my play alone in the deep waters, and I will never be obedient to this son of Adam."'[4] The phrasing of this recalls Adam's own original sin, and

the Eldest Magician/God the Father parallel is played with (but not forced) throughout this tale. Kipling enjoys the extremes of scale, dimension and perspective that the device permits. Pau Amma becomes a figure 'as tall as the smoke of three volcanoes' but the paradox of his situation is that he functions best when he is a very small crab, a tiny creature with effective scissor-like claws. Similar games with dimension and perspective are played in 'The Butterfly that Stamped', where the vast size of the Animal that came out of the sea is to be placed in the context of his family (he is the smallest) while the Butterfly itself, this little winged creature perched on Solomon's forefinger, is found commanding the behaviour of the gigantic 'four gull-winged Djinns' which lift Solomon's Palace the very moment after the Butterfly has stamped.

'The Bridge-Builders' (discussed in chapter 7) balances the world of work against the world of dream and vision. The title of the volume in which it appears, *The Day's Work*, seems to reinforce Kipling's insight (which he shares with Joseph Conrad) that action protects mankind from the nihilism and hopelessness into which we could all otherwise fall. But the creation scene in 'The Crab that Played with the Sea' opens up the opposite possibility. The life of work is a maze in which the imagination is restricted; 'work' and 'play' are polarised terms. J.M.S. Tompkins speaks of Kipling's sense of 'circumfluent mystery', and she finds a striking instance of it in this story. The Eldest Magician, the creator, is telling the newly created animals what they are to play at. 'The elephant is bidden to play at being an elephant, and does so to his own content and that of the Eldest Magician,'[5] and so it is with the rest of the animals, ordered to 'play' at being themselves as the Eldest Magician proceeds with his benevolent act of creation. The Man is treated differently; he is 'too wise for this play'.[6] Nevertheless, the picture and the commentary on it show that the Man has also received an instruction which he must obey.[7] The Maze on which the Man is standing looks like a miniature re-creation of the Palace of Knossos, and the caption raises a question about the significance of this. 'When the Man has done talking with the Eldest Magician he will walk in the Big Miz-Maze, because he has to.'[8]

What is the 'Big Miz-Maze'? In a letter to a literary schoolmaster whom Kipling referred to as a 'younger brother in the craft' of writing, Kipling called the track across the quicksand in 'The Strange Ride of Morrowbie Jukes' (1932) a Miz-Maze, the one route out of the trap into which Jukes has fallen.[9] This sense has carried over into the Crab story where the Miz-Maze is the perilous journey of life itself, as experienced by a normal man. The Man here is set apart from the animals, and he will forget, as Tompkins puts it, 'that he has talked with the Eldest Magician. He will walk in the maze, and darkness and ignorance will be the conditions in which he does his works. The question is always how to get the maximum output out of human stuff, which works best blinkered.'[10]

Though human stuff 'works best blinkered', it is not denied purpose. The Man's life in the Maze finds meaning in action, effectiveness, competence and results: a checklist of the qualities looked for in a young staff officer. A similar checklist often informs Kipling's narratives for adult readers, where competence and results are displayed within a masculine world. In *Kim*, published in 1901 (between *The Day's Work* and *The Just so Stories*, published in 1898 and 1902 respectively), the memorable image of life as a wheel takes up the same theme. Kim's lama seeks to free humankind from the wheel on which we are all bound. The immersion of humans in purposeful activity is thus balanced by the visionary possibilities offered by the gods in 'The Bridge-Builders' as well as by Kim's lama and by the replaying of the creation myth here in 'The Crab that Played with the Sea'.

The Eldest Magician's instruction to his newly created beings is to 'play'. Pau Amma the Crab chooses to dodge the rules of the game.

> Nobody saw him go away except the little girl-daughter where she leaned on the Man's shoulder. And the play went on till there were no more Animals left without orders; and the Eldest Magician wiped the fine dust off his hands and walked about the world to see how the Animals were playing.[11]

In the picture, the mark on the stone under the Man's foot is a 'magic mark'; it is the swastika, a traditional Hindu symbol of good luck, associated with good fortune and Ganesh the elephant god in Hindu culture (as we have seen in Chapter 5). The swastika and the elephant were united in a medallion that John Lockwood Kipling designed for his son. It is reproduced in gilt on the red cloth front board of many of Kipling's books, including the most celebrated (the first edition of *Kim*, for example). The swastika was removed from this image in all Kipling's publications after 1933 because of its association with the Nazis.

The Giant Crab and Other Tales of Old India by W.H.D. Rouse (1897) was a recently published collection of children's stories of which Kipling must have been aware. Rouse's book invites comparison with Kipling's collection, and its new edition of 1900 had delightfully spirited and technically skilful illustrations by Heath Robinson. But Kipling's immediate source was more scholarly than Rouse; he wrote proudly to a friend defending his story of the crab as 'authentic Malay Folklore'.[12] In Kipling's story the Eldest Magician persuades Pau Amma, the giant crab, who is as tall as the smoke of three volcanoes, that he will be better off as a tiny crab which can hide among stones on the sea bed. In this Kipling was following

the version of the crab myth in W.W. Skeat's *Malay Magic* (1900), where 'the Creator of the entire Universe pre-existed by Himself, and he was the Eldest Magician'. This God figure, and the refrain he exchanges with his Muhammad, are closely followed in the Kipling text: 'Kun?' said God, 'Payah kun' said Muhammad, and a seed was created. The seed became a root (lit. sinew), the root a tree, and the tree brought forth leaves. 'Kun?' said God, 'Payah kun' said Muhammad. Then were Heaven and Earth created, 'Earth of the width of a tray, Heaven of the width of an umbrella.'[13]

Kipling brings off the challenging and pleasing task of giving this miniature version of the creation story weight and mass within the compass of a very short text – just 15 or so printed pages in contrast to the more than 700 of Skeat's book. The Eldest Magician visits each of his creatures to ensure that they are well matched to their settings. 'All-the-Turtle-there-was', for example, is 'scratching with his flippers in the sand that had been got ready for him.' The Eldest Magician checks that the Turtle is happy and then 'breathed upon the sand and the rocks, where they had fallen in the sea, and they became the most beautiful islands of Borneo, Celebes, Sumatra, Java, and the rest of the Malay Archipelago.'[14] In Skeat's book there is 'a cavern called Pusat Tassek, or navel of the lake. This is inhabited by a vast crab, who goes forth at stated periods during the day. When the creature returns to its abode the displaced water causes the flow of the tide; when he departs, the water rushing into the cavern causes the ebb.'[15] Kipling's story closely follows these details from Skeat, and his image of Pau Amma the Crab rising out of the sea has an appropriate grandeur. Yet the Crab is helpless because the Eldest Magician has removed his protective shell.

Kipling enjoys creating a rhythmical incantatory prose with which to display the Eldest Magician's power:

He made a Magic with his left hand – with just the little finger of his left hand – and – lo and behold, Best Beloved, Pau Amma's hard, blue-green-black shell fell off him as a husk falls off a cocoa-nut, and Pau

The Crab that Played with the Sea

Amma was left all soft – soft as the little crabs that you sometimes find on the beach, Best Beloved.[16]

The illustration shows the Crab confronted by three human figures in a canoe, the Eldest Magician, naked and statuesque, the Man with his knife, and the Man's daughter.[17] The unprotected Crab is in mortal danger: 'all soft as I am now, the sharks and the dogfish will eat me'.[18] The Crab bargains with the Eldest Magician and with the Man and his little girl-daughter, and all three make him offers: the Eldest Magician promises him safe places in the sea, the Man offers to make him safe on both land

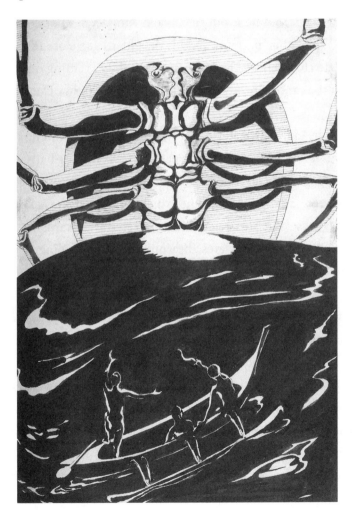

and sea and the little girl-daughter offers him her scissors, which become his claws. The Magician restores his shell with the proviso that he will lose it for one month a year in order to grow a new one. The Crab accepts all these offers and the bargain makes him clawed and hard-shelled. The act of creation is then completed: 'Then the Eldest Magician made a Magic with his right hand, with all five fingers of his right hand, and lo and behold, Best Beloved, Pau Amma grew smaller and smaller and smaller, till at last there was only a little green crab swimming in the water.'[19] The image showing Pau Amma at his full gigantic size has a caption which assures that there is no threat to the Josephine figure: 'Pau Amma is trying to make a Magic, but he is only a silly old King Crab, and so he can't do anything.' The father-narrator and his daughter keep close to each other in complete confidence: 'The Little Girl Daughter is sitting quietly in the middle of the canoe. She knows she is quite safe with her Daddy.'[20]

The sonorous tone of this story invites consideration of Kipling's attitudes to religious faiths. For a short while, back in 1890, Kipling had considered himself 'engaged' to Caroline Taylor, Edmonia Hill's sister. In December 1890 he wrote a letter to Caroline which attempted to make clear his religious views (she suspected him of leanings towards the Roman Catholic Church). He declares disarmingly that Caroline herself is a deity and then unfolds a personal creed:

Chiefly I believe in the existence of a personal God to whom we are personally responsible for wrong doing – that it is our duty to follow and our peril to disobey the ten ethical laws laid down for us by Him or His prophets. I disbelieve directly in eternal punishment for reasons that I would take too long to put down on paper. On the same grounds I disbelieve in an eternal reward. As regards the mystery of the Trinity and the Doctrine of Redemption I regard them most reverently but cannot give them implicit belief, accepting them rather as dogmas of the Church than as matters that rush to the heart. I would give as much to believe in them absolutely [...]. Summarised it comes to *I believe in God the Father Almighty maker of Heaven and Earth and in one filled with His spirit who did voluntarily die in the belief that the human race would be spiritually bettered thereby.* I believe after having seen and studied eight or nine creeds in Justification by work rather than faith, and most assuredly do I believe in retribution both here and hereafter for wrong doing as I believe in a reward, here and hereafter for obedience to the Law.[21]

If this was actually designed to persuade Caroline, then it backfired; she probably found his rejection of 'the dogmas of the Church' alarmingly heretical. In any case, elusive as quicksilver, Kipling was rapidly moving away from the world to which Caroline belonged. The year 1890 had been the *annus mirabilis* for Kipling, the year in which he burst upon the literary scene in London with wholly original subject matter and a new and unique voice.

The whole hasty business of his brief engagement to Caroline is an instance of the impulsiveness and emotional instability which characterised him as a young man, and would resurface at intervals throughout his life. A much later letter, written from Chartres to his close friend Rider Haggard in 1925, revisits these speculations about the truth or otherwise of Christian doctrine (or the doctrine of any faith, for that matter). He refers to medieval windows (like those of Chartres cathedral) in the language of a man who seeks religious certainty but knows that he is unlikely to find it. 'Colour, old man, is what au fond clinches a creed. Colour and the light of God behind it. That's as near as Man will ever get.'[22] There is longing here, but no more than that. His certainties, where they can be felt, are rooted in loyalty to human communities and institutions rather than to any religious doctrine. In *Kim* he discriminates between the Roman Catholic chaplain, Father Victor, who is presented with considerable sympathy, and Bennett, the Church of England army chaplain who is obtuse and foolish. The strongest respect for a priest-like figure, though, is reserved for the lama's absolute commitment to Buddhism in this novel.

How the *Just so Stories* Were Made

Angus Wilson's enthusiasm for the first seven stories in the *Just so* volume makes one wish that he had discussed more fully the three later tales, 'The Crab that Played with the Sea', 'The Cat that Walked by Himself' and 'The Butterfly that Stamped'. They are the longest in the volume, the most elaborately worked, the most consciously literary and the most ambitious. Also they bring a different perspective to the talking animal stories as Kipling practised them, for in them the animals accommodate themselves respectively to a Magician, to a human family and to Solomon. The story of the Cat 'that walks by himself' is the most intimate and personal of the three.

11

THE CAT THAT WALKED
BY HIMSELF

Hear and attend and listen; for this befell and behappened and became and was, O my Best Beloved, when the Tame animals were wild. The Dog was wild, and the Horse was wild, and the Cow was wild, and the Sheep was wild, and the Pig was wild – as wild as wild could be – and they walked in the Wet Wild Woods by their wild lones. But the wildest of all the wild animals was the Cat. He walked by himself, and all places were alike to him.

Of course the Man was wild too. He was dreadfully wild. He didn't even begin to be tame till he met the Woman, and she told him that she did not like living in his wild ways. She picked out a nice dry Cave, instead of a heap of wet leaves, to lie down in; and she strewed clean sand on the floor; and she lit a nice fire of wood at the back of the Cave; and she hung a dried wild-horse skin, tail-down, across the opening of the Cave; and she said, 'Wipe your feet, dear, when you come in, and now we'll keep house.'[1]

'The Cat that Walked by Himself' belongs to the period between 1896, when the Kiplings left Vermont and made temporary homes on the British south coast, and 1902, the year in which they found a permanent home in Sussex. While house-hunting the Kiplings travelled round Sussex in their 'locomobile', an ostentatiously expensive (and unreliable) steam-driven vehicle which reflected Kipling's new-found love of mechanised personal transport. In 1900 they found Bateman's, a sturdy historic house near

Burwash, which appealed to them. Kipling's biographer Charles Carrington described what happened next:

> It was a well-built square Jacobean house of stone in a lonely valley, at the foot of a steep lane running down from an unfrequented village. 'Bateman's' took their fancy so that for three days they talked of little else, but while they hesitated, someone stepped in and rented it. That was in August 1900, and nearly two years passed before they heard that 'Bateman's' was vacant again.[2]

This time Kipling did not hesitate. He was able to write excitedly on 30 November 1902 to his friend Charles Eliot Norton:

> Behold us lawful owners of a grey stone lichened house – AD 1634 over the door – beamed, panelled, with old oak staircase, and all untouched and unfaked. Heaven looked after it in the dissolute times of mid-Victorian restoration and caused the vicar to send his bailiff to live in it for 40 years, and he lived in peaceful filth and left everything as he found it.[3]

Earlier, Lockwood Kipling had spelled out for Sarah Norton the emotional background to the Kiplings' inability to settle happily in England. Any house they looked at would be empty of Josephine.

> Rud and Carrie, I may confide to you and Mr Norton who love them, found going back to the 'Elms' much harder and more painful than they had imagined. The house and garden are full of the lost child and poor Rud told his mother how he saw her when a door opened, when a space was vacant at table, coming out of every green dark corner of the garden, radiant – and heart breaking. They can talk of her, however, which is much, for Carrie has hitherto been stone-dumb. But to Mrs K she softened and broke forth and they had long discourse, mingling their tears as women may and mothers must.[4]

The Cat that Walked by Himself

'Hear and attend and listen', the first imperative phrase in the 1902 text of 'The Cat that Walked by Himself', was not in the story as first published in the *Ladies' Home Journal*. The added phrase reminds us that the stories were written to be read aloud, and its resonant tone is drawn from Kipling's memories of his childhood visits to the Burne-Jones cousins at The Grange in London, 'where the family would read Lane's *Arabian Nights* and parody that author's modes of address in the manner taken up in the *Just so Stories* – "Best Beloved" or "O Enemy and wife of my Enemy." '[5] 'The Cat that Walked by Himself' and 'The Butterfly that Stamped' were the last two stories to be completed before the whole book was sent to the publisher. It embodied, as Andrew Lycett says, 'another Kipling paradox – a children's book with an enduring, magical tone that was the opposite of the raucous antics of Stalky only three years earlier'.[6] Reviewers were mystified. In an attempt to identify the genre to which they belonged G.K. Chesterton wrote that they were 'like fairy tales told to men in the morning of the world'.[7]

'Wipe your feet, dear,' gives an affectionate nod of recognition to Carrie's domestic control. The Woman uses her skills to tame the Wild Man. She makes 'wild sheep roasted on the hot stones, and flavoured with wild garlic and wild pepper; and wild duck stuffed with wild rice and wild fenugreek and wild coriander; and marrow-bones of wild oxen; and wild cherries and wild grenadillas. Then the Man went to sleep in front of the fire ever so happy.'[8] Once he is asleep the Woman makes 'the First Singing Magic in the world'.[9] Singing had been a source of consolation to Kipling as a child. His autobiography describes his Goanese *ayah* singing nursery songs, and his mother sang as well, and accompanied herself on the piano.[10]

In the Crab story the Eldest Magician was the initiator of all 'play', including, we must assume, all human cultural activity. In the Cat story immediately following, the Woman is originator and the creative force. Among the animals the Dog is the first to take the bait, surrendering to the smell of the roast mutton 'for I think it is good'. The Cat refuses to join him. 'I am the Cat who walks by himself, and all places are alike to me. I will not come.' 'Then we can never be friends again,' says Wild Dog.[11] The story is based partly on the Kiplings' early years in Vermont and partly on their winter holidays in South Africa at The Woolsack. His homes were of great emotional importance to Kipling, and two of them are relevant to this story. The landscape through which the Cat walks in the first image is recalled from views from Naulakha at Brattleboro.

Kipling's daughter Elsie recalled her father composing some of the stories in The Woolsack. He would read them aloud, and if the children came up with suggestions that he liked he would adopt them and incorporate them into the text. He also worked on the illustrations 'with meticulous care', she wrote, 'and was delighted when we approved of the results'.[12] Their South African holidays were among the happiest episodes in their lives for both Carrie and Rudyard Kipling. With John and Elsie they stayed there to avoid the English winter each year until 1908. Beyond that date Kipling became disenchanted with South Africa for political reasons; he had fervently hoped that it would develop into an exclusively British colony, but the complicated settlements following the South African War left it a republic to be shared between the British and the Dutch. The Woolsack, though, made available to him by Cecil Rhodes, retained a special place in his heart, and he retained his title to it for the rest of his life. Literary friends like Henry James had done their best to remind him that he was primarily a writer and that he ought to be faithful to his craft, but his position now was that the British Empire was a force for good in the world and that he was making himself useful by actively promoting it. His identity was becoming bound up with it. He enjoyed the company of men who exercised power and influence, and with whom he felt at home in his London clubs.

The plate in which the Cat walks 'by his wild lone through the Wet Wild Woods' shows the creature stalking down an ordered avenue of trees – far from 'wild' in its design – which recalls the Vermont setting of the Kiplings' first home. The caption tells us that nothing grows in the wild woods except toadstools: 'they had to grow there because the woods were so wet'. Beneath the main image, in the predella, is the 'cosy Cave that the Man and the Woman went to after the Baby came'. The landscape here actually looks like an American farmland scene from Vermont. It includes a jovial young horseman 'holding up his hand to call the Dog',[13] confident as he rides back to the cave. This recalls the Kipling family when it was just three people, Kipling, Carrie and Josephine, and the horseman is clearly Kipling himself. But the confidence with which he rides and raises his hand in a big generous gesture could also recall Beatty Balestier, with whom Kipling had been on good terms before their disastrous quarrel.

There is a sad postscript to the story of Beatty, set out with balance, clarity and appropriate generosity by Birkenhead:

It is, at least, a melancholy satisfaction to have heard from Beatty's second wife that in the later years all hatred of Kipling had vanished from his mind, and that his restless spirit was at last cleansed from revengeful thoughts. Indeed it is doubtful if he had ever really harboured them. He never relaxed his hostility to his sister, to whom he attributed the whole disaster. When he was dying, worn out by the mad impetus of his life, with the writs at last pouring in, he said with pathetic impotence that if ever Kipling came back he would be his best friend – he would get all the bands in Brattleboro to play for him. [...] He died in poverty and debt at Brattleboro in 1936, the same year in which Rudyard Kipling was buried in Westminster Abbey.[14]

'The Cat that Walked by Himself' is a story about successfully making a home, domesticating an environment and establishing a safe place for a family. It is in the same imagined era as the 'Neolithic' Taffimai stories. The story takes it as given that the man in the cave, Wild Man, needs to be tamed. The Woman makes 'magic' over a blade-bone, and the story's first initial, the H of 'Hear and attend and listen', is an image of the blade-bone, which is itself inscribed with runes.

Kipling put painstaking detail into his runes. They contain embedded jokes about writing, which do take some unpacking. The runes read: 'I Rudyard Kipling dreu this but because there was no mutton bone in the house I faked the anatomy from memori. R. K.' Further runes on the crosspiece of the H read: 'I also urote all the plais ascribed by Mrs Gallup'.[15] In 1900 Mrs Gallup had published an account of what she took to be codes in Shakespeare's texts, which she interpreted as showing that they were written by Sir Francis Bacon, the sixteenth-century scientist, philosopher and statesman who served both Queen Elizabeth and James I. Kipling's story 'The Propagation of Knowledge' (in *Debits and Credits*, 1926) has

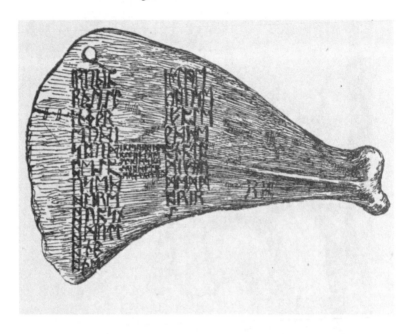

a group of schoolboys teasing the Baconians, and his much more serious story, 'Dayspring Mishandled' (1932), has a forged Chaucerian fragment as the centre-piece of a story about love and revenge.

Kipling the writer resembles the Cat, always independent in his own mind and professional life regardless of his external circumstances. The caption to the second image brings out Carrie's domesticity. The picture shows 'really a very nice Cave, and much warmer than it looks'. The caption adds that 'All those little smudges on the sand between the Cave and the river are the marks of the Woman's feet and the Man's feet. The Man and the Woman are both inside the cave eating their dinner. They went to another cosier Cave when the Baby came, because the Baby used to crawl down to the river and fall in, and the Dog had to pull him out.'[16] Kipling is perhaps deflecting the memory of Josephine here by making this first baby a boy rather than a girl.

His daughter Elsie wrote a memoir of her parents which somewhat reinforces the notion that Kipling's marriage to Carrie could be hard going at times:

The Cat that Walked by Himself

> [Carrie's] possessive and rather jealous nature, both with regard to my father and to us children, made our lives very difficult, while her uncertain moods kept us apprehensively on the alert for possible storms. There is no doubt that her difficult temperament sometimes reacted adversely on my father and exhausted him, but his kindly nature, patience, and utter loyalty prevented his ever questioning this bondage, and they were seldom apart.[17]

To Kipling's utter loyalty one may add his comfortable dependency on Carrie. Harry Ricketts quotes an engaging little cameo from earlier in the marriage when the Kiplings were still living in Vermont. They were setting out for a trip to New Jersey, and their friend and neighbour Mary Cabot asked them which hotel they would be staying at. Kipling replied, 'Why, bless you, I don't know! I am no more than a cork on the water, when Carrie is with me.'[18] Living away from England had suited Carrie very well, as she could keep her distance from Alice Kipling, her mother-in-law. They were destined never to get on, though their emotional detachment was temporarily broken down by the death of little Josephine. After displaying massive, indeed frightening, self-control during those terrible weeks following Josephine's death in New York, Carrie and Alice had both wept when Carrie, Rudyard and Elsie were back in Rottingdean. But the rapprochement did not last. The older Kiplings never fully forgave Carrie's power over their son, and in England Carrie avoided her parents-in-law as much as she could. South Africa was an escape from all that. There she had her husband and the children to herself.

Carrie was fond of cats. In this respect among many others 'The Cat that Walked by Himself' is a story for Carrie. She is the woman who is making bargains with her animal visitors, she is the maternal force which has tamed the Wild Man, she attends to the comfort of the cave and ensures that it is a place of warmth, food, domesticity and child-rearing. The story indicates the best aspects of Carrie: her conscientious and hard-working nature, and her dedication to her husband's and children's well-being. Human wit and agency triumph in both 'The Butterfly that Stamped' and 'The Cat that Walked by Himself'. In the Butterfly story the vanity of the males (the Butterfly and Solomon) is exposed by the wisdom of their respective wives; and in the Cat story the cat thinks he is himself the victor, but it is a Pyrrhic victory; he will for ever have a home in the cave by the woman's favour but the Dog and the Man remain free to persecute him. It is a nice balance.

For Kipling, one special appeal of Bateman's, the cave-like home which resonates engagingly with the Cat story, had to do with his genuine delight in historical places. Some workmen arrived offering to dig a well for the house, and in *Something of Myself* Kipling invested them with supernatural and timeless properties:

> Then, out of the woods that know everything and tell nothing, came two dark and mysterious Primitives [cousins, then, of Tegumai in 'How the First Letter was Written']. They had heard [about Kipling's desire for a well]. They would sink that well, for they had the 'gift'.[19]

They dig down until 'at twenty-five feet we had found a Jacobean tobacco-pipe, a worn Cromwellian latten spoon and, at the bottom of all, the bronze cheek of a Roman horse-bit'. These findings, and advice from his cousin Ambrose Poynter, prompted the writing of the time travel fantasies in *Puck of Pook's Hill* and *Rewards and Fairies*. Kipling's interest in the history of Bateman's was at least in part a matter of putting down roots and establishing a personal relationship with rural Sussex and its people. The local peasantry lived in a landscape which recedes into the remote past.

Carrie had put up with the discomforts of Bliss Cottage in the first year of her marriage, and was obliged now to put up with the difficulties of moving into an old building with multiple problems. As soon as they became owners of Bateman's Kipling went away on a trip leaving Carrie to sort out the contractors, builders, plumbers and electricians who were working on both the house and the surrounding property, which was extensive. He would engage himself with the technical stuff, though, because that interested him. Adapting the eighteenth-century watermill which belonged to Bateman's in order to generate an electricity supply for it was a major enthusiasm for him. As far as the day-to-day management of his life was concerned, Kipling was content to leave the details to this well-organised woman who was devoted to his comfort. Henry James and others saw the marriage as one in which Kipling was Carrie's prisoner, his movements, friendships and range of activities sharply circumscribed by her, but this was a misreading. The Cat's self-will and self-possession are Kipling's behaviour as a writer, and the Cat outwits the Woman. This quietly tells us that Kipling saw himself as triumphant in such power struggles as there were within his marriage. The Woman says to the Cat 'we have no more need of either friends or servants in our Cave' (Carrie prided herself on her skill in hiring and managing her servants). The Cat here, interestingly, displays his own capacity for aggression: 'Cat grew very angry and said, "Has wild Dog told tales of me?"' And the Woman, the Carrie-figure, dismisses him: 'You are neither a friend nor a servant. You have said it yourself. Go away and walk by yourself in all places alike.'[20]

The Cat gets the better of the Woman by flattery, telling her, 'You are very wild and very beautiful.' (This invites a comparison between the Woman's petit-bourgeois competence and the selfless wisdom of Queen Balkis in the next story, 'The Butterfly that Stamped'.) The Woman is beguiled into making her unwise promise: if she says one word in the Cat's praise he may enter the cave, if she says two he may sit by the fire, if she says three he can have milk every day. His opportunities to meet these requirements are provided by the new baby. The Cat plays with the baby, then diverts its attention by playing with a spindle, and then kills a mouse. The Woman praises him for each service, and an eternal bargain is struck between these two natural enemies. The Cat will remain on hostile terms with Men and Dogs ('three proper Men out of five will always throw things at a Cat whenever they meet him, and all proper Dogs will chase him up a tree') but the Cat's truce with the Woman remains firm. Kipling's matrimonial bargain with Carrie involved a degree of subservience balanced by a degree of independence, and both parties to the contract understood that. 'The Cat that Walked by Himself' can be read as a gentle tribute to Carrie Kipling's competent domestic management.

'The Cat that Walked by Himself' was written late in the sequence of the stories, January 1902, and therefore was conceived and composed in the full glow of the publication of *Kim* and the satisfying reception of that masterpiece. *Kim* is an inexhaustibly rich text, yielding fresh resonance and significance with each rereading, and its central figure has characteristics in common with Kipling's Cat. The Cat reflects on his own independence of action ('all places are alike to me'),[21] and Kim, similarly, reflects on his own identity, roles and autonomy. Two older men offer him absolute love. Mahbub Ali the Pathan horse dealer is an orthodox Muslim, a Sunni, who is working with a British officer, Creighton, to employ Kim in British intelligence in India, and Venerable Teshoo Lama, the Buddhist monk, claims Kim as his *chela*, his companion, in his quest for the River of the Arrow of Buddhist tradition. Kim values both these relationships, but like the Cat in the *Just so* story, he hesitates to commit himself.

Mahbub Ali urges Kim to exploit his multiple identities. 'Among Sahibs, never forgetting thou art a Sahib; among the folk of Hind, always remembering thou art –';[22] and there Mahbub Ali pauses. A central question in *Kim* is where he belongs, what he is, which faith he follows. 'What am I? Mussalman, Hindu, Jain, or Buddhist? That is a hard nut.'[23] Mahbub has no answer to this, and falls back on relationships, rather than creed, as a way in which Kim can define himself: 'Thou art also my Little Friend of all the World, and I love thee.' He then has an exchange with Kim which opens up the tensions between their loyalties and exposes Mahbub's simple and open jealousy of Kim's attachment to the lama.

'I say in my heart the Faiths are like the horses. Each has merit in its own country.'

'But my lama said altogether a different thing.'

'Oh, he is an old dreamer of dreams from Bhotiyal. My heart is a little angry, Friend of All the World, that thou shouldst see such worth in a man so little known.'

'It is true, Hajji; but that worth do I see; and to him my heart is drawn.'

Mahbub acknowledges the unique, precious nature of this friendship: 'Friend of all the World,' said Mahbub [...] 'I have met many men, women, and boys, and not a few Sahibs. I have never in all my days met such an imp as thou art.'[24]

Mahbub is a complex figure and a master of dissimulation, but in this scene he drops his guard and displays his emotional openness in relation to the Irish boy. To this extent he compares with the Dog in 'The Cat that Walked by Himself'. The Dog commits himself wholly to the family in the cave: 'Wild Dog crawled into the Cave and laid his head on the Woman's lap, and said, "O my Friend and Wife of my Friend, I will help your Man to hunt through the day, and at night I will guard your Cave."' The Cat at this point reflects: '"That is a very foolish Dog." And he went back through the Wet Wild Woods waving his wild tail, and walking by his wild lone. But he never told anybody.'[25]

Anna Balestier, Carrie's mother, had a reputation as a daunting matriarch, but both she and Carrie displayed commendable stoicism and resilience in the face of personal tragedy. When Wolcott Balestier died from typhoid fever in Dresden on 6 December 1892, Henry James wrote that: 'Poor little concentrated passionate Carrie [was...] remarkable in her force, acuteness, capacity, and courage – and in the intense, almost manly nature of her emotion. She is a worthy sister of poor dear big-spirited, only-by-death-quenchable Wolcott.'[26] There is no mention of Wolcott's death in *Something of Myself*. This is not necessarily a signal that the friendship was forgotten. It is more likely that the pain of this loss was such that Kipling chose not to resurrect his memories of Wolcott for his memoir.

As Wolcott's nephew, John Kipling, grew into a leggy adolescent, taller than Rudyard, he reminded the family of Wolcott. Anna Balestier's fond letters to John remind us that the boy was half American. He was conscious of his own looks, spending money on clothes and gramophone records and the like, as young people do, and pleased with the sporting achievements he could chalk up at Wellington. In December 1911, Kipling wrote to Anna Balestier to say that John had difficulty accepting the idea that his father was 'a sort of public man'. 'They ask him at school if he had read any of his father's books and he says quite truthfully "no"'. Kipling is filled with pride by his son's physical development ('back from school, growing like a corn stalk, with a cracked voice and a great taste in clothes!'). In the same letter he brought out the American side of John's nature: John was 'a humorous chap. Now and then he reminds me of Wolcott, in the speed and accuracy of his repartees'.[27]

Later, in March 1915, after John Kipling had joined the Irish Guards and was clearly likely to be sent to the front in France, a former French governess to the family asked Kipling a simple question which must have touched a nerve: why, if there was 'no compulsion', had John joined the army? Carrie Kipling had a prepared script to deal with this question. She said firmly that he had enrolled precisely '*because* there was no compulsion'.[28] Anna Balestier also wondered how it was that Carrie and Kipling could have the courage to send her grandson off to a situation in which he was highly likely to be killed. Carrie replied: 'There is nothing else to do. The world must be saved from the German who will worse than kill us all if he is allowed a chance and one can't let one's friends' and neighbours' sons be killed in order to save us and our son. There is no chance John will survive unless he is so maimed from a wound as to be unfit to fight. We know it and he does'.[29] This echoes the mindset of that whole generation of parents steeling themselves for the worst. For his part, John Kipling was delighted to volunteer for military action; he was 'an entirely typical specimen of the young men who rushed to arms in 1914 at their country's call'.[30]

The Cat that Walked by Himself

As Hugh Brogan has pointed out, neither John Kipling nor his father committed themselves to the war irrationally. Brogan writes that Kipling 'was not silly, or even unrepresentative'. He 'knew, as did everyone else of his time, that Britain was dependent on sea-power and sea-trade not merely for the preservation of her empire, but for survival'.*[31] Their long-standing friend Rider Haggard met the Kiplings in London early in 1915 and reported that 'Neither of them looks so well as they did. Their boy John, who is not yet eighteen, is an officer in the Irish Guards and one can see that they are terrified lest he should be sent to the front and killed, as has happened to nearly all the young men they knew.'[33]

John Kipling grew in confidence and personality during the period of his military training, and he wrote letters which displayed wit and self-assertion. His period as a soldier filled his parents' hearts with pride. On 17 August 1915, his birthday, John wrote to his parents from 'somewhere in France'. On 25 September he and his battalion received orders to move to the trenches near Loos, with the certainty that they would go 'over the top' on the following day: 'funny to think one will be in the thick of it tomorrow', he added. 'This will be my last letter most likely for some time.'[34] On 2 October his parents received a War Office telegram to tell them that John was 'missing and wounded'.[35] The reality was that he had become separated from his company, had been caught perhaps by a solitary sniper, and had died in agony with half his head shot away. Within a few weeks of the telegram Kipling wrote to his friend Lionel Dunsterville (the model for 'Stalky') indicating that his son had to be

---

* In this essay Hugh Brogan also works to rebalance the broader judgements on the causes of the war: 'The First World War was such an appalling disaster that there can only be one verdict on the European generation that brought it about: they failed scandalously in an essential duty and must be blamed, but they must also be pitied. For although it can hardly be denied any longer that it was the wanton decisions of Austro-Hungary and Germany which made the great tragedy inevitable, all the other powers had made mistakes in the years before the war and all were to suffer horribly. So although it is still difficult for us, our task is not to take sides, but to understand. Such a cool approach will help us to appraise Kipling better than either retrospective jingoism or retrospective pacifism.'[32]

presumed dead. 'It was a short life. I'm sorry that all the years' work ended in the one afternoon but – lots of people are in our position and it's something to have bred a man.'[36]

While Kipling could expose his immediate anguish to an old friend in this way, for their acquaintance at large he and Carrie kept open the possibility that John had been taken prisoner and was still alive. But then on 6 October 1915, the Kiplings saw this in the *Morning Post*:

> We have the heavy burden of announcing that Mr John Kipling, of the Irish Guards, is reported 'missing, believed killed.' John Kipling was the child for whom his father wrote the *Just so Stories*, the boy for whom Puck told immortal tales of the beloved land, for which this supreme sacrifice has now been made.

Kipling did not need the reminder that he had now lost two of his children, and further flatfooted and tactless observations included a reference to John's 'delicate health' and a painful, true, statement that John's parents had offered 'the dearest of all possible sacrifices on the altar of their country' when John need not have volunteered for military service at all. He was an 'only son, whose youth and health might have given them good reason for avoiding the ordeal.'[37] The piece was by H.A. Gwynne, editor of the *Morning Post*, and it had been written with the best intentions. Gwynne was a friend of the Kiplings and he had been on very good terms with young John Kipling, which deepened the hurt. John's battalion had inaccurately told Gwynne that he was listed as 'wounded, believed killed', whereas the official listing for him read 'wounded: missing.'[38]

For at least another year Kipling's public position on this remained that his son's death had not been confirmed. In 1916 Kipling reacted to a letter from the War Office saying that John must now be regarded as dead by writing that he had been 'wounded and left behind' and that 'no one saw him killed.'[39] Hoping against hope, Kipling pursued many avenues of enquiry (including the Swedish royal family's direct contact with the

Kaiser). Carrie recalled John on the day he left for the front: he was looking tall and handsome in his uniform. 'Send my love to Daddo' was his parting message to the father who loved him and was proud of him.[40]

Kipling had been suffering for a while from unexplained stomach pains. He had an undiagnosed ulcer, and this began to trouble him seriously immediately following this disaster, and caused him pain, sometimes acute, for the rest of his life. In the months following John's death it was variously described by doctors as 'gastritis' and 'indigestion', but in 1916 Kipling himself attributed it to 'the strain and anxiety caused by the disappearance of our son'.[41] In his ballad 'My Boy Jack', Kipling's own grief is transposed and spoken by a bereaved mother about her drowned sailor son. It is one of the most haunting of all the poems to come out of the Great War:

'Have you news of my boy Jack?'
Not this tide.
'When d'you think that he'll come back?'
Not with this wind blowing, and this tide.

'Has anyone else had word of him?'
Not this tide,
For what is sunk will hardly swim,
Not with this wind blowing, and this tide.

'Oh, dear, what comfort can I find?'
None this tide,
Nor any tide,
Except he did not shame his kind –
Not even with that wind blowing, and that tide.

Then hold your head up all the more,
This tide,

And every tide,
Because he was the son you bore,
And gave to that wind blowing and that tide![42]

By November 1918 the waste and pointlessness of John's death were brutally apparent. On Armistice Day, when the whole nation took stock following the struggle of the preceding four years, Carrie Kipling's diary entry is heartbreaking in its restraint: 'Rud and I feel as never before what it means now the war is over to face the world to be remade without a son.'[43]

12

THE BUTTERFLY THAT STAMPED

This, O my Best Beloved, is a story – a new and a wonderful story – a story quite different from the other stories – a story about The Most Wise Sovereign Suleiman-bin-Daoud – Solomon the Son of David.

The last three stories in the 1902 *Just so Stories* volume are among Kipling's strongest work. The fresh approach to the creation myth in 'The Crab that Played with the Sea' and the elegantly played out clash of strong wills (with its tribute to Carrie) of 'The Cat that Walked by Himself' continue to stake out claims for Kipling's originality and power. 'The Butterfly that Stamped', the twelfth and final story in the 1902 edition of the *Just so Stories*, proclaims itself as a new kind of story. It neither offers further alternatives to the biblical creation myth, nor instructs the child in the nature of strange lands and remote societies:

There are three hundred and fifty-five stories about Suleiman-bin-Daoud; but this is not one of them. It is not the story of the Lapwing who found the Water; or the Hoopoe who shaded Suleiman-bin-Daoud from the heat. It is not the story of the Glass Pavement, or the Ruby with the Crooked Hole, or the Gold Bars of Balkis. It is the story of the Butterfly that Stamped.[1]

In the initial letter of this story, Solomon, or Suleiman, is illustrated as a figure of leisure and grandeur, and the imagery of Freemasonry, in

which Kipling look a life-long interest, has contributed to his identity. Suleiman is not only supreme in the world of men; like Mowgli from the *Jungle Books*, he can communicate with all the animals and birds. He also speaks to the earth itself:

> He understood what the beasts said, what the birds said, what the fishes said, and what the insects said. He understood what the rocks said deep under the earth when they bowed in towards each other and groaned; and he understood what the trees said when they rustled in the middle of the morning. He understood everything, from the bishop on the bench to the hyssop on the wall.[2]

What is a *bishop* doing in this list (beyond the neat assonance of 'bishop' and 'hyssop')? That is not an entirely frivolous question. The Anglican church of Mrs Holloway's devotions in horrible Southsea had been a grimly suburban institution, and the Methodist church of Kipling's grandparents has no bishops. Freemasonry, by contrast, was an institution that Kipling loved and admired, and Suleiman's splendour is closely associated with it. Kipling's invention here draws on the Old Testament narrative of the building of the temple of Jerusalem under King Solomon as it is given in the King James Bible (II Chronicles: 2–5). The narrative in 2 Chronicles details the magnificence, opulence and dazzling extravagance of Solomon's creation, as for example in this passage about the decoration of the Temple:

> He made the most holy house, the length whereof was according to the breadth of the house, twenty cubits, and the breadth thereof twenty cubits: and he overlaid it with fine gold, amounting to six hundred talents. And the weight of the nails was fifty shekels of gold. And he overlaid the upper chambers with gold. And the wings of the cherubim were twenty cubits long: one wing of the one cherub was five cubits, reaching to the wall of the house: and the other wing was likewise five cubits, reaching to the wing of the other cherub. (II Chronicles 3:8–11)

Kipling's illustrations to his story include huge Djinns, whose scale reflects the vast cherubim in II Chronicles. And in Kipling's image of King Suleiman himself within the historiated initial, the letters on his sash read HTWSSTKS, which refers to the building of Solomon's Temple; they evoke 'the Mark Mason's song' of which the first line is 'Hiram, the Widow's Son, sent to King Solomon the great Key Stone.' This relaxed, all-powerful patriarch is reclining in a golden throne designed to resemble the wings of griffins, and redolent also of the ceremonial chair used during the installation of the Master and Officers of a Masonic Lodge. Further, Suleiman is wearing a bracelet with the Masonic emblems of a square and a pair of compasses.[3]

Kipling is lightly touching on his own success here. A Master in Freemasonry resembles one aspect of the Kipling who had become a world-famous writer; no longer the young literary lion who had taken the world by storm in 1890, but a more seasoned and established version of the same man. *Kim*, published in the previous year, was recognised as his unassailable masterpiece. He was buying the country house which became his permanent home in England, and although he famously and scrupulously turned down most offers of public honours, he was, nevertheless, adopting a lifestyle of some grandeur. Kipling had, by all the criteria of his day, 'arrived', and the story of the Butterfly may be taken as a gentle reminder to himself of the temptations of success and the shallow lure of vanity.

Like the Cat story, the Butterfly story explores the power balance within a relationship between a man and a woman, but here the emphasis is quite different. The indirect reference to Carrie's strong-mindedness which can be detected in the Cat story is replaced here by admiration for a woman's ability to enable a man to acknowledge his own strengths. It takes further the cunning displayed by the Woman in 'The Cat that Walked by Himself'. Male power is balanced by a woman's long-sighted patience.

The story plays with the kind of outrageous hyperbole which is guaranteed to amuse a small child. Suleiman, we are told,

> married ever so many wives. He married nine hundred and ninety-nine wives, besides the Most Beautiful Balkis; and they all lived in a great golden palace in the middle of a lovely garden with fountains. He didn't really want nine hundred and ninety-nine wives, but in those days everybody married ever so many wives, and of course the King had to marry ever so many more just to show that he was the King.[4]

The meetings between Suleiman, or Solomon, and the Queen of Sheba are described in I Kings 10:1–13 and II Chronicles 9:1–12. The biblical Solomon and the Queen of Sheba were not married, but in Kipling's story they are. The Queen is not named in these Old Testament texts, but she is named as 'Balkis' in Arabic sources. The poet Robert Browning, with his delight in the recondite and obscure, knew this, and his 1883 poem 'Solomon and Balkis' may well have provided the colouring of the characters for Kipling. In Browning's poem, Solomon is tricked into acknowledging that the driving force in his own life is vanity, and in the Kipling story Suleiman acknowledges vanity as a failing in himself which must be conquered. Kipling's Balkis is a clever altruist while Browning's is an earthier figure propelled by lust. She seeks the company of good men: 'Provided the Good are the young, men strong and tall and proper,/Such servants I straightway enlist.' Browning's Queen then breaks off, with blushes; she has said too much.[5] Kipling also clearly enjoyed the version of their story given in a recently translated Islamic source of which he owned a set, the 'Rauzat-Us-Safa', or Garden of Purity (published by the Royal Asiatic Society, in two volumes, in 1892). Here 'Suliman' and the Queen 'Balquis' are much drawn to each other, though never married, and the great sexual attractiveness of Balquis is given in detail, as are the astonishing wealth and fabulous power enjoyed by Suliman.

The prelude to the Butterfly story has claimed that its subject matter is entirely 'new', but it seems fair to place it with the Cat story and read it as another fable in which Kipling ponders the nature of marriage. Suleiman is much pestered by the quarrelling of his nine hundred and ninety-nine wives. As a generous joke designed to help his friend the Butterfly, Suleiman ensures that when the Butterfly stamps 'his left front forefoot', four huge Djinns will make his palace disappear. Suleiman becomes an accomplice in the taming of the Butterfly's wife, who is laughing at her husband. Suleiman promises that 'she will never laugh at you again':

he turned the ring on his finger – just for the little Butterfly's sake, not for the sake of showing off, – and, lo and behold, four huge Djinns came out of the earth! 'Slaves,' said Suleiman-bin-Daoud, 'when this gentleman on my finger (that was where the impudent Butterfly was sitting) stamps his left front forefoot you will make my Palace and these gardens disappear in a clap of thunder. When he stamps again you will bring them back.'[6]

Kipling's audience of small children would have longed for Suleiman to exercise his power over his wives. But he will not. 'Of course if he had chosen to turn his ring on his finger and call up all the Djinns and the Afrits they would have magicked all those nine hundred and ninety-nine quarrelsome wives into white mules of the desert or greyhounds or pomegranate seeds'; but Suleiman-bin-Daoud 'thought that would be showing off. So, when they quarrelled too much, he only walked by himself in one part of the beautiful Palace gardens and wished he had never been born.'[7] He walked by himself, like the Cat, but the woman in his life can ensure that Suleiman's happiness will be restored to him. Balkis' plan comes to a successful conclusion. 'At last Suleiman-bin-Daoud will do for the sake of a Butterfly what he ought to have done long ago for his own sake, and the quarrelsome Queens will be frightened!'[8]

As he wrote the caption to 'the picture of the four gull-winged Djinns lifting up Suleiman-bin-Daoud's Palace the very minute after the Butterfly had stamped', Kipling was clearly pleased by the ingenuity of the image: 'The Palace and the gardens and everything came up in one piece like a board, and they left a big hole in the ground.' The caption points us to the tiny figures, lower right in the main image, of Suleiman-bin-Daoud with his magic stick and the two butterflies hovering behind him. In the predella is another Djinn, of a quite different kind, 'a very friendly Djinn called Akraig. He used to feed the little fishes in the sea three times a day.' He has no part in the story. 'I put him in to show you what a nice Djinn is like.'[9]

Kipling's account of 'the Animal that came out of the sea and ate up all of the food that Suleiman-bin-Daoud had made ready for all the animals in all the world' is drawn directly from *The Garden of Purity*.[10] In this source text Suleiman's munificence is for 'all the tribes of men, genii, birds, fishes, and to all the creatures of God'. But 'the Divine Will'

demonstrated its own greater 'omnipotence and grandeur' by sending a single sea-creature which ate the whole of the banquet.[11] In Kipling's story, Suleiman makes an arrogant gesture, but he has over-reached himself and is confounded:

> He very seldom showed off, and when he did he was sorry for it. Once he tried to feed all the animals in all the world in one day, but when the food was ready an Animal came out of the deep sea and ate it up in three mouthfuls. Suleiman-bin-Daoud was very surprised and said, 'O Animal, who are you?' And the Animal said, 'O King, live for ever! I am the smallest of thirty thousand brothers, and our home is at the bottom of the sea. We heard that you were going to feed all the animals in the world, and my brothers sent me to ask when dinner would be ready.'[12]

The Animal declares that what he has eaten already was no more than a between-meals snack, and Suleiman then forswears the exercise of magic. In Kipling's image the creature is domesticated: the caption tells us that the Animal which 'ate up all the food' was 'really quite a nice animal',[13] and indeed his head is that of an impossibly enlarged and ugly, but friendly, seal. The Islamic source's hyperboles are engagingly reflected and gently mocked: 'His Mummy was very fond of him and of his twenty-nine thousand nine hundred and ninety-nine other brothers that lived at the bottom of the sea. You see he was the smallest of them all, and so his name was Small Porgies.'[14]

'The Butterfly that Stamped' points outwards to the high importance that Freemasonry had held for Kipling since his own admission to the Craft. For Kipling the satisfactions of Freemasonry were deep. It was exclusively male, classless, benevolent and secretive. Kipling became a Freemason in Lahore, at the Lodge of Hope and Perseverance No. 782, when he was 'under age' (he was elected in April 1886 and would not reach the age of 21 until December of the same year). He and his father worked on the visual appearance of the building: 'I helped, and got the father to advise, in decorating the bare walls of the Masonic Hall with hangings after the prescription of Solomon's Temple.' He was elected young because the lodge hoped for a good secretary.*

Freemasonry is important in *Kim*. Kimball O'Hara's Irish father, a former colour-sergeant of an Irish regiment, is a member of the same Masonic lodge, 'The Lodge of Hope and Perseverance, no. 782 E.C.' ('E.C.' stands for 'Excellent Companion'). The observances and rituals of Freemasons would in due course contribute to 'In the Interests of the Brethren', 'The Janeites' and 'A Madonna of the Trenches', collected in *Debits and Credits*.

I have referred above in my discussion of 'The Sing-Song of Old Man Kangaroo' to 'The Man who would be King', first published in *The Phantom Rickshaw* (1888). Dravot and Carnehan, two former British soldiers turned adventurers, make themselves the effective rulers of a region called 'Kafiristan' which is imagined as part of a frontier region between India and Afghanistan. They introduce themselves to the narrator, the young Kipling in his newspaper office, as 'Brother Peachey Carnehan' and 'Brother Daniel Dravot' (they are 'Brothers' in that they are Freemasons). Knowledge of the craft has enabled them to take possession of their remote kingdom by persuading the inhabitants that they are descendants of Alexander the Great (a tradition in Freemasonry) and are therefore gods. Their power is absolute until Dravot betrays his lack of divinity by forming a relationship with a woman. She bites him, he bleeds, and his common humanity is exposed. The people dispose of him and

---

* When he joined the Freemasons, Kipling associated himself with a strong and rapidly growing institution. The Lodge of Hope and Perseverance No. 782 was one of the largest lodges, founded in 1858 (the year after the Indian Mutiny). In 1886, the year that Kipling joined, there were twenty-two Masonic lodges in the Punjab with some 600 members in all. Kipling became secretary to the lodge the following year, 1887. Andrew Lycett considers that Freemasonry helped Kipling to find a balance between his outer and his inner selves, 'between his professional advancement and emotional development'.[15]

then crucify Carnehan, whose horribly damaged hands, witnessed by the narrator at the end of this story, testify to his ordeal.

Much later, in *Debits and Credits*, Kipling presented a group of stories urging the consolations of Freemasonry for men broken by the Great War. The strongest of these tales, written in 1917, is 'In the Interests of the Brethren'.[16] It features former soldiers finding comradeship and a comforting structure among their fellow Masons. As Kipling wrote in his autobiography, Freemasonry brought him into contact with 'Muslims, Hindus, Sikhs, members of the Araya and Brahmo Samaj [Hindu communities], and a Jew tyler [the doorkeeper at a Masonic Lodge], who was priest and butcher to his little community in the city [Lahore]. So yet another world opened to me which I needed.'[17] It helped to free the young man from the little fortresses of Englishness which the British masters of India tended to create for themselves, and it furnished him with a moral code. 'Masonry,' as Lycett puts it, 'with its ethical and metaphysical elements, provided the nearest equivalent to a coherent belief system for a young man who, for all his knowingness, was still floundering to make sense of India's mass of conflicting creeds.' Though not himself religious, Kipling 'was fascinated by the way in which religions sought to explain the more complicated issues of human existence'. India was, for Kipling, 'a spiritual bazaar', and he 'needed a philosophy with an intellectually satisfying explanation of the world and its mysteries'. Freemasonry provided that. Further – and this is directly relevant to the Masonic references in 'The Butterfly that Stamped' – its basic tenets lead back 'to Solomon's construction of the Temple in Jerusalem, referring frequently to precise units of measurement'.[18] Work, craft, and Kipling's natural delight in making detailed beautiful things ingeniously and slowly, found moral and social sanction in Freemasonry.

In 'In the Interests of the Brethren', the Master of the Masonic Lodge is a tobacconist named Burges. (Kipling gives Burges common ground with himself; Burges has lost his only son in the war.) Burges's lodge is a 'Lodge of Instruction', and as its Master Burges is committed to the maintenance of ritual for the benefit of its members. 'All Ritual is fortifying. Ritual's a natural necessity for mankind. The more things are upset, the more they fly to it. I abhor slovenly Ritual anywhere.'[19] One of the men, shell-shocked and silent, is dressed by a friend for the lodge's ceremony:

> 'Someone in front of me tightened a belt on a stiffly silent person in civil clothes with discharge-badge. 'Strewth! This is comfort again,' I heard him say. The companion nodded. The man went on suddenly: 'Here! What're you doing? Leave off! You promised not to! Chuck it!' and dabbed at his companion's streaming eyes.
>
> 'Let him leak,' said an Australian signaller. 'Can't you see how happy the beggar is?'
>
> It appeared that the silent Brother was a 'shell-shocker'.[20]

The damaged man can release his emotions by weeping with happiness once he is wearing the Masonic apron. The lodge master's commitment to ritual feels here like a conviction which was both personal and valuable for Kipling.

'A Madonna of the Trenches' and 'The Janeites', also in *Debits and Credits*, pay further tribute to the healing and cherishing that Freemasonry could offer to damaged soldiers. 'A Madonna of the Trenches' is both a story of Freemasonry serving as a safety-net for a distraught soldier, and a ghost story, the form that Kipling had perfected early in his life with his Indian tale 'The Phantom Rickshaw'. In 'A Madonna', a young soldier, Strangwick, from a South London lodge, comes to the attention of the Senior Warden of Lodge Faith and Works E.C. 5837. Keede is a doctor in civilian life, who struggles to understand Strangwick's mental health; Strangwick has 'the Jumps to the limit'[21] but hides the real trauma that has damaged him. There is a backstory, rooted in a close-knit working-class London community. Strangwick's aunt, 'Auntie Armine, Ma's younger sister',[22] is in a relationship with a soldier, John Godsoe, who in civilian life is a close friend and neighbour of Strangwick's family. Auntie Armine has sent a message to 'Uncle John', who is serving in the trenches: 'I expect to be through with my little trouble by the twenty-first of next month, and I'm dyin' to see him as soon as possible after that.'[23] The conventional idiomatic phrase harbours a literal truth: Auntie Armine is dying of breast cancer. Uncle John understands the message and kills himself with charcoal fumes on the appointed day. Strangwick sees the ghosts of the two lovers united in the corpse-lined trench at the front in which Uncle John is serving. Death from cancer was very much in Kipling's mind in 1923, when he wrote this story; the gastric illness from which he had suffered since the death of his son John in 1915 gave him constant pain in this year, and he believed that cancer was the cause.

'The Janeites' brings out the value of Freemasonry by obliquely comparing it with another secret society, in this case a group of British soldiers in the Great War who use their knowledge of Jane Austen's novels as their common bond. Kipling's point here is that the nature of the common ground is less important than the fact of the healing community that it creates. The central comedy of the story turns on the touching figure of Humberstall, a giant innocent who has 'no more touched liquor than 'e 'as women since 'e was born,'[24] as one of the soldiers puts it. Humberstall has been traumatised and confused after nearly losing his life when an ammunition dump at Étaples in northern France exploded, but he has nevertheless managed to return to the front to be with his community of Janeites. Although he lives in a world of gentle delusion, the Janeites remain loyal to him.

Debits and Credits ends with 'The Gardener', the story in which Kipling most directly confronts his grief over the loss of his son. In the early spring of 1925 Rudyard and Carrie Kipling visited the Imperial War Graves Commission Cemetery at Rouen, where 11,000 war graves represent what Kipling called 'the shock of this Dead Sea of arrested lives.'[25] The following day he began to write 'The Gardener'. In this tale an Englishwoman, Helen Turrell, from the polite, restrictive society of an English village, goes to

France to look for the grave of her 'nephew' Michael Turrell. Her neighbours in the village have guessed that this 'nephew' is in fact Helen Turrell's illegitimate son, whom she passes off as the child of her brother George Turrell, 'a retired non-commissioned officer' who had 'died of a fall from a horse a few weeks before his child was born'.[26] In the final pages of the story Helen visits the cemetery, not expecting that it 'counted twenty-one thousand dead already'. She has no way of knowing which is Michael's grave. 'She went forward, moved to the left and the right hopelessly, wondering by what guidance she should ever come to her own.' She receives help: 'A man knelt behind a line of headstones – evidently a gardener, for he was firming a young plant in the soft earth.' He asks who she is looking for. The story then moves boldly into the realm of the supernatural and the biblical:

'Lieutenant Michael Turrell – my nephew,' said Helen slowly and word for word, as she had many thousands of times in her life.[27]

The man lifted his eyes and looked at her with infinite compassion before he turned from the fresh-sown grass toward the naked black crosses.

'Come with me,' he said, 'and I will show you where your son lies.'

When Helen left the Cemetery she turned for a last look. In the distance she saw the man bending over his young plants; and she went away, supposing him to be the gardener.[28]

This is a quotation from John 20:15 in the King James Bible. Helen has met the risen Christ. This straightforward presentation of a miracle in modern times is the most daring of Kipling's confrontations with Christianity.

Craftsmanship (in addition to the 'Craft') is central to Kipling's perception of his own identity as a writer. His soldier ballads, especially 'Danny Deever', had made him a sensation in 1890, and his versatility as a poet is striking. Dramatic monologues, especially 'The Mary Gloster' and 'McAndrew's Hymn', demonstrate the aptitude with which he had learnt from Browning's use of the form, and his poetry of the Great War, some of which is a direct heartfelt response to the death of John Kipling, compares strongly with the work of the acknowledged major 'War Poets' Owen, Sassoon and Rosenberg.

In each of Kipling's collections of stories the shape and balance of the volume are carefully considered. This is not obvious; the reader has to work at each collection in order to grasp the structure in Kipling's mind. Thus, in *Debits and Credits*, the opening and closing stories are adaptations of biblical narratives. 'The Enemies to Each Other' is a stylistic experiment, telling the story of the fall of Adam and Eve in the manner of the *Tales of the Arabian Nights*, and 'The Gardener', where Kipling indirectly confronts the loss of his own son, is based, as we have seen, on the story of Mary Magdalene encountering the risen Christ. The titles of the volumes can also be riddling. 'Traffics and discoveries' is a deliberately obscure quotation from the title page of Hakluyt's *Travels* (1589). The balance of contrasting nouns in his double titles, *Traffics and Discoveries*, *Debits and Credits* and *Limits and Renewals*, points to, but does not explain, what he believed his art could and could not do. The books for children which followed the *Just so Stories* – *Puck of Pook's Hill* and *Rewards and Fairies* – also have these features.

Despite all the strengths of Kipling the artist, he has long been experienced as a reprehensible and problematic figure. This debate was already well under way nearly 80 years ago: in his well-known 1942 essay on Kipling, George Orwell remarked that 'during five literary generations every enlightened person has despised him' – but these commentators are 'forgotten' while Kipling 'is in some sense still there'.[29]

By 1900 Kipling's friend Cecil Rhodes had become a Solomon of his age, who controlled the South African diamond industry and founded the immodestly named 'Rhodesias' as British possessions. The Kipling who mocks Solomon's grandiose claim to omnipotence in 'The Butterfly that Stamped' was, in public life, a man who admired the equally grandiose ambitions of his friend. During the years 1898–1902, while he was still writing his balanced, witty and self-contained fables for children, Kipling was also committing himself to a political allegiance which pulled him into explicitly racist writing. His friendship with Rhodes was cut short by the latter's death from heart failure at the early age of 49 on 26 March 1902. But the impact of Rhodes was permanent.[30]

Humphrey Carpenter wrote that Kipling stood alone among children's writers in that he 'straddled' two streams of children's literature, the 'breezy, optimistic adventure story' of figures like G.A. Henty, and the 'Arcadian' fantasy writing of Kenneth Grahame and A.A. Milne.[31] There was a hunger for narratives of overseas adventure in the 1880s and 1890s, an appetite fed by Kipling's friend Rider Haggard as well as by Stevenson and Conrad, and Kipling benefited from the expectations created by their excursions into exotic and inaccessible parts of the world. But in a late Victorian context, the adventure story genre easily shades into a defence of imperialism, and it was this more than anything else that harmed Kipling's literary reputation. His audience grew steadily between 1880 and 1898, but resistance began to build in response to his support for Britain's war with the Dutch in South Africa after 1899, and by 1910 his reputation was damaged, and would remain damaged. His attitudes to Africans were quite different from his personal interest in Indians. He fully endorsed Rhodes' imperial ambitions in Africa, and there can be no doubt that during his many visits to South Africa he saw Africans as did his friend Rider Haggard: as alien 'others' living in a world which the white man was entitled to control. Kipling is one of the targets of Edward Said's blistering account, in *Orientalism*, of the white man's authority 'before which non-whites, and even whites themselves, were expected to bend', an agency 'for the implementation of policy towards the world within which the impersonal communal ideal of being a White Man ruled'.[32]

After the successful publication of *Kim*, Henry James, with his unrivalled commitment to artistic purity, tried to persuade Kipling to turn his back on his political activities, but in vain. James was clearly right about what would be best for his friend. The public life to which

Kipling increasingly committed himself after 1908 would in due course disappoint him.[33] Increasingly, in the latter years of the Edwardian decade, Kipling felt that he was living in a country which had become strange to him. His deep emotional investment in Bateman's is like that of Henry James in English country houses. Richard Gill wrote about this aspect of James that it was 'the most favoured emblem of all, the most repeated figure in the Jamesian carpet'. In James' work the English country house was a ' "local habitation" for many of his own values; a unifying focus to which his multitudinous impressions of the good life might gravitate'.[34] Kipling's feeling for physical and historical England was similar. This was partly a matter of compensation for other losses: the 'family square' was breaking up, and his sister Trix had made a dull marriage, was childless, and began to show signs of mental illness. Alice Kipling did her best to help her daughter, whose sanity became increasingly fragile. Kipling's wish to help his sister was restricted because Carrie and Alice Kipling, both strong-willed women, found it temperamentally difficult to cooperate with each other.

Lockwood Kipling visited Bateman's regularly; Alice tended to stay away. She developed a condition called Graves' disease and died late in 1910. Lockwood Kipling died a couple of months later. Trix, now schizophrenic, reinforced the split between her mother and Carrie, claiming that Carrie had prevented Kipling from looking after his parents, and then she developed a hatred of her brother, claiming that he had cheated her out of her inheritance.[35] The Neolithic family that Kipling created in his *Just so Stories*, with the strong bond between father and daughter, looked increasingly ironic as the brutal realities of life and death forced themselves upon him with the passage of time.

13

THE TABU TALE AND HAM AND THE PORCUPINE

The most important thing about Tegumai Bopsulai and his dear daughter, Taffimai Metallumai, was the Tabus of Tegumai, which were all Bopsulai.

'The Tabu Tale' was collected only in the American edition of the *Just so Stories* published by Scribner. This third tale about Tegumai and his daughter Taffimai belongs to an older phase of children's literature in that it is about the value of obedience, though at the same time it echoes *Stalky & Co.* to the extent that it celebrates sturdy independence and self-determination. What it has in common with the other Neolithic stories is its endorsement of the support to be gained from membership of a family and a tribe.

We learn that when Taffimai 'went out into the woods hunting with Tegumai, she never kept still. She kept very unstill. She danced among dead leaves, she did. She snapped dry branches off, she did. She slipped down banks and pits, she did [...] and she made a horrible noise!'[1] She interrupts the hunting on which her father is quietly intent and then like a well-behaved and polite child says, 'I'm awfully sorry, Daddy, dear.'

Then Tegumai said: 'What's the use of being sorry? The squirrels have gone, and the beavers have dived, the deer have jumped, and the rabbits are deep in their buries. You ought to be beaten, O Daughter of Tegumai, and I would, too, if I didn't happen to love you.' Just then he saw a squirrel kinking and prinking round the trunk of an ash-tree, and he said: 'H'sh! There's our lunch, Taffy, if you'll only keep quiet.' Taffy said: 'Where? Where? Show me! Show!' She said it in a raspy-gaspy whisper that would have frightened a steam-cow, and she skittered about in the bracken, being a 'citable child; and the squirrel flicked his tail and went off in large, free, loopy-leps to about the middle of Sussex before he ever stopped.[2]

Punishment of children in the *Just so Stories* has no chance of turning ugly, and in this story Taffy's penalties are imagined in a rapidly *descending* order of severity. 'He stood quite still, making up his mind whether it would be better to boil Taffy, or skin Taffy, or tattoo Taffy, or cut her hair, or send her to bed for one night without being kissed.'[3] The Head Chief of the Tribe consults Tegumai about a sanction for the whole tribe to prevent over-fishing of the river. The sanction will take the form of a tabu. The consequence of breaking the tabu will be 'sticks and stinging-nettles and dobs of mud; and if *that* doesn't teach them, we'll draw fine, freehand tribal patterns on their backs with the cutty edges of mussel-shells'.[4] The Head Chief of the tribe has a tabu pole set by the river to forbid fishing for six months, and he allows Taffy her own tabu to protect her garden. He also confers a tabu on Tegumai, so that he can halt Taffy at will if he sees her in danger. He gives Taffy one of his own magic necklaces; it will activate a tabu if Taffy hangs it 'on anything that belongs to your own self'.[5] Taffy hangs it to protect the entrance to her garden outside the family's cave. Three tabus thus come into play: for Tegumai, so that he can halt Taffy at will; for Taffy, enabling her to control trespassers in her own garden; and for the whole tribe, to conserve the fish.

The code thus adopted is challenged when Tegumai himself breaks Taffy's tabu:

He lifted Taffy's bucket with the tabu-necklace on it. Next minute he fell down flat on the floor and shouted; then he curled himself up and rolled round the cave; then he stood up and flopped several times. [...] He took three sorrowful steps and put his head on one side, and shouted 'I broke tabu! I broke tabu! I broke tabu!'[6]

The shaking of the code does not end there: the Head Chief himself is also trapped by the tabu in Taffy's garden and has to perform the same penance. These tabus have a serious purpose, as does the 'law of the jungle' taught to Mowgli in the two *Jungle Books*. Taffy's life is saved when her father is able to halt her in her tracks and then kill a wolf which is following her. The story ends with affectionate male roughhousing, a form of celebration closure with which Kipling was always comfortable. When Taffy goes to bed 'Tegumai and the Head Chief came in to say goodnight, and they romped all round the cave, and dragged Taffy over the floor on a deerskin.' The Carrie figure in the story, Taffy's mother, stops the fun, as one might expect: 'Still! Still Tabu on every one of you! How do you ever expect that child to go to sleep?'[7]

Kipling's image of the totem referred to in the story is carefully worked. The caption repeats a joke from 'The Elephant's Child' where Kipling pretended not to know the names of some of the animals he had drawn: 'That fat thing at the top is the Tribal Beaver of the Tribe of Tegumai.' The totem pole is elaborate: 'Below the Beaver are four birds – two ducks, one of them looking at an egg, a sparrow-bird, and a bird whose name I don't know. Below them is a Rabbit, below the Rabbit a Weasel, below the Weasel a Fox or a Dog (I am not quite sure which), and below the Dog two Fishes.'[8] The totem is a 'fish tabu', a warning from the Head Chief that fishing must be suspended for a period. Kipling had read the discussion of totems and 'tabus' in J.G. Frazer's *The Golden Bough* (1890), and he recorded that his story, based on the 'totem tales', was written in October 1898. He had visited the Native American collections at the Smithsonian Institute in Washington DC, and the images in the story and the notion of the 'tabu' are drawn from the examples of Native American culture that he saw there.

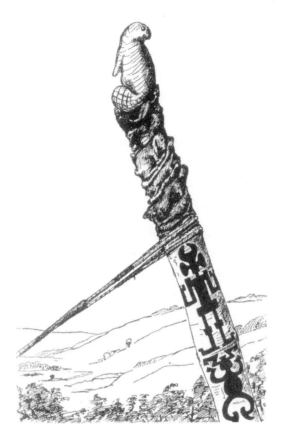

The story is about training, and is somewhat in the mood of his friend Robert Baden-Powell's *Scouting for Boys* (1908). Kipling had collaborated with Baden-Powell to a minor degree, allowing him to use the episode involving Lurgan and the jewels (from chapter 9 of *Kim*) in a chapter called 'Kim's Game' designed to train Scouts in the skills of observation and recall.[9] Baden-Powell's brief account of *Kim* selects from Kipling's novel the skills that the boy Kim has which are valuable to the British Empire. Lurgan, the jeweller who is also a member of the British government's intelligence department in India, makes use (in Baden-Powell's words) of Kim's 'special knowledge of native habits and customs', which make him 'a useful agent for Government Intelligence work, that is, a kind of detective among the natives'. A key part of the training – both for Kim and, as Baden-Powell sees it, for the Scouts – is in 'strong-mindedness'. Lurgan found Kim 'strong-minded and quick at learning' and then gave him lessons in noticing small details and remembering them, 'which is a most important point in the training of a scout'. Baden-Powell flattens the story of *Kim* in such a way that very little of Kipling's creation is left. For him, Kipling's masterpiece is noteworthy for Kim's skills, his use of disguise, and his useful friendship with his lama ('a holy priest').[10]

The 'Neolithic' setting of the three Tegumai and Taffimai stories invites comparison with Kipling's fantasies based on the history of England, *Puck of Pook's Hill* and *Rewards and Fairies*. Like his near contemporary E. Nesbit in *Five Children and It*, *The Phoenix and the Carpet* and *The Story of the Amulet*, Kipling used fantasy to summon figures from the past to tell their stories. This works well where the figures become friends of the child characters and reappear in several of the stories (like Parnesius, a Roman centurion from the time of Hadrian). The best-written of these stories, 'The Tree of Justice' (in *Rewards and Fairies*), has only a very slight relation with historical probability. Harold, the Saxon King, has survived the Norman Conquest and, as a very old man, 40 years after his supposed death, is an unrecognised pilgrim at the court of the Norman King Henry I. He is protected by the King's jester, Rahere, who resembles Shakespeare's truth-telling Fool in *King Lear*, 'more of a priest than a fool and more of a wizard than either'.[11]

The second additional *Just so* story, 'Ham and the Porcupine', was composed much later in Kipling's life and published in *The Princess Elizabeth Gift Book in aid of the Princess Elizabeth of York Hospital for Children* (1935). It was written in response to a letter he received from a child asking how the porcupine got his spines. The Kipling who wrote this was an ill and disillusioned man. Two of his own children were by this date dead, and it would be the last year of his own life. Still, he could respond to a personal appeal from a child.

The Tabu Tale and Ham and the Porcupine

In 'Ham and the Porcupine' the animals from the story of Noah are being prepared by Ham, one of the sons of Noah, to take refuge in the Ark. The creatures are, perhaps, to be thought of as toys.

> When All the Animals lived in Big Nursery, before it was time to go into the Ark, Big Nurse had to brush their hair. She told them to stand still while she did it or it might be the worse for them. So they stood still. The Lion stood still and had his hair brushed into a splendid mane with a blob at the tip of his tail. The Horse stood still, and had his hair brushed into a beautiful mane and a noble tail. The Cow stood still and had her horns polished, too. The Bear stood still and got a Lick and a Promise. They all stood still, except one Animal, and he wouldn't. He wiggled and kicked sideways at Big Nurse.[12]

This one animal is the Porcupine, and the Porcupine develops his spines rather as the Elephant's Child had developed his trunk in the earlier tale – through disobedience. The Porcupine refuses to stand still and have his hair brushed, so 'Big Nurse' gives up with an impatient curse: 'On-your-own-head-be-it-and-all-over-you!'[13] The spines accordingly grow all over the Porcupine. He becomes 'fretful' and injures Ham's legs with his spines.

Ham, the darkest-skinned of Noah's sons and mythical ancestor of all the black peoples of Africa, is a robust and attractive figure. He defends his dignity in his dialogue with the Porcupine:

> 'Just because a man looks a little sunburned and talks a little chuffy, don't think you can be fretful with him. I am Ham! The minute that this Dhow touches Mount Ararat, I shall be Emperor of Africa from the Bayuda Bent to the Bight of Benin, and from the Bight of Benin to Dar-es-Salam, and from Dar-es-Salam to the Drakensberg, and from the Drakensberg to where the Two Seas meet round the same Cape. I shall be Sultan of Sultans, Paramount Chief of all Indunas, Medicine

Men, and Rain-doctors, and specially of the Wunungiri – the Porcupine People – who are waiting for you. *You* will belong to me! You will live in holes and burrows and old diggings all up and down Africa, and if ever I hear of you being fretful again I will tell my Wunungiri, and they will come down after you underground, and pull you out backwards. I – amm – Hamm!'[14]

The Porcupine's destiny will be to live in holes and burrows under threat of punishment from Ham, while his gentle cousin the hedgehog will 'fetch up in a comfy little place called England – all among gardens and box-borders and slugs, where people will be glad to see you.'[15] The hedgehog is worried that he, too, may have to live underground, but Ham spares him this fate:

He touched the small Hedgehog Brother with his foot, and Hedgehog curled up – which he had never done before.

'Now you'll be able to pick up your own dry-leaf bedding on your own prickles so you can lie warm in a hedge from October till April if you like. Nobody will bother you except the gipsies; and you'll be no treat to any dog.'

'Thank you, Sir,' said small Hedgehog Brother, and he uncurled himself and went after more black beetles. And it all happened just as Ham had said.[16]

Ham's prospect of becoming the 'Emperor of all Africa' recalls Chaka, King of the Zulus, from Haggard's *Nada the Lily*. The notion that Ham is a royal figure recalls the sympathetic portrayal of the Ethiopian in 'How the Leopard got his Spots', and is a further corrective to the negative perception of Africans which characterised some of the references to them elsewhere in Kipling's writing.

'Ham and the Porcupine' marks a valediction to the travelling that Kipling had enjoyed for much of his life. His last voyage was made in the first months of 1931, when he and Carrie sailed to Egypt and up the Nile as far as Aswan, returning in May. After that, his undiagnosed ulcer, which caused him constant pain, put further extended travel out of the question. The 'comfy little place called England' was embodied for him by the security of his own house, Bateman's, and its surrounding land. Kipling had had a prodigiously hard-working and productive life, but since the loss of his son in the Great War he found himself living in a world that he did not understand and in which he had no influence. In March 1924 he wrote to Rider Haggard, inviting his old friend to join him in shared regret. Every man 'looks back with a half-broken heart on the failure of all the things he has tried to bring about in his life'.[17]

EPILOGUE

The *Just so Stories* were appropriately timed. Their writing and publication were concurrent with a rich surge of fresh original writing for children, and a striking new confidence in the writers. Kenneth Grahame's two best-selling books about childhood, *The Golden Age* (1895) and *Dream Days* (1898), helped create the climate in which his own *The Wind in the Willows* (1908), with the river as its idealised setting and the strong friendship of Ratty and Mole at its heart, met with striking commercial success. Kipling's *Just so Stories* contributed to this climate, and in their year of publication, 1902, Beatrix Potter published *The Tale of Peter Rabbit* and E. Nesbit brought out *Five Children and It*. Potter's Peter Rabbit would feature in five more of her books, while the 'It' of Nesbit's title (a creature which looks like a toad but is actually a Psammead or 'sand fairy') appears in two further titles, *The Phoenix and the Carpet* and *The Story of the Amulet*. The Psammead and the Phoenix are both miracle-working creatures who can grant wishes, the consequences of which in many of the stories are unwelcome. 'Be careful what you wish for' is their implicit watchword, as it is also in Kipling's 'The Sing-Song of Old Man Kangaroo', where the Kangaroo gains useful legs but is left hopelessly hungry.

The ground had been prepared by Lewis Carroll, whose fantasies for children were exhilaratingly free of the moral teaching which had tended to dominate British children's books in the first half of the century. Elements of this moral seriousness survived in works like Kingsley's *The*

Epilogue

Water-Babies (1863) and Margaret Gatty's *Parables from Nature* (1888), but the *Alice* books swept all that aside. Alice stands up to controlling adults like the Caterpillar and the Queen of Hearts, and the fantasy follows its own logic by making her a Queen in the chess game which closes the second book. There is exhilarating energy in writing for children in the latter part of the century.

What is the place of the *Just so Stories* in English literature and culture, both in the early twentieth century and now? As a model they have been taken up recently in the *Just When Stories* (2010), a volume of animal stories the point of which is to ask 'just when will these creatures become extinct?' These tales bring out the imminent threat of extinction to species. William Boyd's vivid and compact tale is of a young man releasing an organ-grinder's monkey from its captivity. Michael Morpurgo's piece is a spare and vivid account of a stranded turtle being saved by a small boy and an old woman.[1] Antonia Michaelis contributes a giant tortoise story which is close in method to Kipling's talking animal tales. In this story, Lonesome George, the sole survivor of a giant tortoise species on the Galapagos Islands, talks to a visiting scientist. He has learnt where there is a female of his own species so that it would be possible for the species to be saved from extinction if they mated, but he feels too old, comfortable and complacent to be bothered.

Talking animals remained a staple of books for small children throughout Kipling's lifetime. In *The Wind in the Willows*, Mole is helped by the more experienced Rat to negotiate the layered nature of a social world which is new to him, and in A.A. Milne's *Winnie the Pooh* (1926) and *The House at Pooh Corner* (1928) the stuffed animal figures reflect recognisable social types (Piglet and Pooh are securely middle class, Eeyore feels ill-housed and excluded, Owl has ancestors he can boast about, Kanga and Tigger are exotic newcomers from Australia and India respectively). These stories have had a constant readership since the volumes were first published (and an authorised modern collection of Winnie the Pooh stories by David Benedictus was published in 2009).[2]

How the *Just so Stories* Were Made

The talking animal stories of the late nineteenth and early twentieth centuries were partly to do with a healthy appetite among publishers for good-quality illustrated children's books of all kinds. George Macdonald's *The Princess and the Goblin* (1871) and *The Princess and Curdie* (1883) found large and enthusiastic audiences among children, as did Edward Lear's publications. Lear's ambition was to be taken seriously as a landscape painter (and indeed he was a very good one), but his *Book of Nonsense* (1846) sold better than his paintings and merited further editions in 1855 and 1861. It was followed by similar titles such as *Nonsense Songs* (1871), *Nonsense Stories* (1871) and *More Nonsense* (1872), and it is for the technical virtuosity of such nonsense poems as 'The Owl and the Pussycat' (1871) and its accompanying illustrations that he is now famous. He died in 1888, and the growing popularity of his nonsense writing coincided with Kipling's childhood and teenage years.

Kipling never recovered from the death of seven-year-old Josephine in 1899. He knew the pain of this bereavement to be endless, and it is reflected in a letter written in 1900 to a young friend, the journalist Brimley Johnson, about a quite different bereavement. Johnson had been engaged to marry a girl who had worked for the Kipling family as a nurse and governess until her sudden, cruelly modern death, killed by a bus while riding her bicycle. Kipling offered to Johnson 'such comfort as men say time brings after loss. It's apt to be a weary while coming but one goes the right way to get it if one interests oneself in the happiness of other folk, even though the sight of this happiness is like a knife turning in a wound.'[3]

Kipling had opened himself emotionally to Josephine in a way that he did not achieve with his two younger children, Elsie and John, although Elsie is actually the 'person small' who asks a myriad questions in the closing poem to 'The Elephant's Child'. In his day-to-day social behaviour Kipling was guarded and self-protective, masking deep feeling behind a clubman's male facetiousness. His professional life was (literally) enclosed and disciplined; in America Carrie stationed herself at his study door to keep visitors away. Josephine's death resonates in the tale of Pau Amma the Crab (where she is the observant little girl who notices the crab scuttling away), and it underlies all three of the Taffimai and Tegumai narratives. It was a deep and lasting source of grief, an experience so appalling that from the day she died he was a changed man. His surviving daughter, Elsie, wrote of Josephine that 'She belonged to his early, happy days, and his life was never the same after her death; a light had gone out that could never be rekindled.'[4]

'The Brushwood Boy', a supernatural story written several years before the tragedy of Josephine's death, became linked with 'They' (see Chapter 9) by the circumstances of its publication. This story presents a central figure, George Cottar, whose dreams from childhood to adulthood involve a girl figure whom he meets on a beach, and as an adult he meets and marries this dream girl in reality. This fantasy was placed as the last story in *The Day's Work* (1895), which may be taken as indicating that it has special personal significance for Kipling, although it is not in itself a strong story. It is in part a parable about perfect masculinity, embodied in its protagonist, and in that respect it is continuous with the themes of *Stalky & Co.* and *The Light that Failed*. And, like 'They', this fantasy develops a conservative pastoral perception of England. The two stories were collected together in a sumptuous edition, with Townsend's illustrations, by Macmillan in 1925.

Surprisingly, the brilliant subversive intellectual H.G. Wells adopted the conservative pastoral vision of England for one of his most widely read novels. *The History of Mr Polly* is a cheerful farce in which a failing small shopkeeper burns down his own shop and finds fulfilment in a pastoral world where he helps out in a country pub. Both *The History of Mr Polly* and *The Wind in the Willows* subscribe to the Edwardian fixation with the English landscape as the positive embodiment of 'Englishness'. I have explored this theme in a previous book:

The History of Mr Polly (1910) is in all senses a more 'innocent' novel than its predecessors. Lewisham and Kipps become men: Mr Polly moves retrogressively through the story until he becomes a child-like, plump figure – Mr. Toad without the mischievousness – sitting by the stream at the Potwell Inn, enclosed in a womb. The valley of the Potwell Inn lies [as Wells writes] 'as if everything lay securely within a great, warm, friendly globe of crystal sky. It was as safe and enclosed and fearless as a child that has still to be born.'[5]

In the Edwardian period writers across the political spectrum were attracted by settings which were insulated from the violence of the world. A striking example is the country house which gives its name to E.M. Forster's *Howards End* (1910): initially expressing the aggressive materialist values of the Wilcox family, it will in due course, once Margaret Schlegel takes possession of it through her marriage to Henry Wilcox, become a bastion of liberal humanism.[6] The security represented by such settings was threatened, obviously, by the fear of international conflict, which is reflected in the 'invasion novels' of the period 1890–1914. Some of these took the kind of martial masculinity with which Kipling's name was increasingly associated as a touchstone. George Chesney's *The Battle of Dorking: Reminiscences of a Volunteer*, in which Britain is defeated and occupied by the Germans, is told from the perspective of an old man who recalls the invasion of England by the Germans some 50 years in the past. First published as a pamphlet by *Blackwood's Magazine* in 1871, *The Battle of Dorking* was revived in 1914 as a warning to the nation. In its introduction by G.H. Powell – in effect, part of the recruitment drive of Lord Roberts, a friend of Kipling, in support of the war – Kipling is cited in support of the pamphlet's revival: the British had adhered to 'a humane aversion to War', and 'Mr Kipling has sung long since of athletic excesses and indolence.'[7]

This is a reference to 'The Islanders', the poem of 1902 in which Kipling had rebuked his contemporaries for assuming that they were unassailable and inviolable.

No doubt but ye are the People – your throne is above the King's.
Whoso speaks in your presence must say acceptable things:

Epilogue

Bowing the head in worship, bending the knee in fear –
Bringing the word well smoothen – such as a King should hear.

Kipling was very angry in this poem. For the South African War the English had sent unfit and untrained men to fight:

Sons of the sheltered city – unmade, unhandled, unmeet –
Ye pushed them raw to the battle as ye picked them raw from
the street.

The arrogance of the English went further still: the mother country had effectively turned its back on the problems in its dominions:

Then ye returned to your trinkets; then ye contented your souls
With the flannelled fools at the wicket or the muddied oafs at
the goals.

In this view the English are more interested in the upper-class and public-school pursuits represented by organised games than they are in actually winning a war:

Will ye pitch some white pavilion, and lustily even the odds,
With nets and hoops and mallets, with rackets and bats and rods?
[...]
Arid, aloof, incurious, unthinking, unthanking, gelt,
Will ye loose your schools to flout them till their brow-beat
columns melt?[8]

'Gelt' – castrated – is a particularly ferocious word. It is extraordinary that this attack on the state of the nation and the figures who failed to lead it was published in the same year as Kipling's *Just so Stories*. A split was opening up between the public perception of the two Kiplings, the creative writer and the political activist. His hardening into that latter role was in part an understandable response to international events but it was also intimately connected with his private grief; it was a way of continuing to deal with the loss of Josephine.*

A particularly weird instance of the invasion genre is a 'romance' by M.P. Shiel called *The Yellow Danger* (1898), in which the threat of invasion by the Chinese is defeated by skilled British seamanship which ensures that much of the population of China is swallowed up in a whirlpool. This triumph of genocide tips over into a kind of apocalyptic madness: 'Twenty million straight and fluttering pigtails, keeping ever their distances, race in narrowing whorls towards a bottomless, staggering well.'[10] This is followed by a political realignment as a result of which Britain commands the whole planet: 'England, no doubt, *will*, in truth, absorb the world; the Loadstone [*sic*] is within us.'[11]

Kipling had actually written something comparable to this, surprising though that may seem, in 'Letters of Travel' (collected as *From Sea to Sea*, 1901). He included a piece regretting that China was not (yet) a British possession. The British could have given the Chinese 'the painful pushing forward, and studious, even nervous, regard of their interests and aspirations that we have given to India';[12] therefore, he concludes, 'you have conquered the wrong country. Let us annex China.'[13] The same frame of mind underlay his support in this period for compulsory military service (he beat this particular drum steadily throughout the Edwardian decade and beyond). By 1912 he had become a noisy personal supporter of Lord Roberts' pressure for the introduction of national

---

* Harry Ricketts quotes a lampoon from C.L. Graves' and E.V. Lucas' *Lives of the Lustrous* (1901) in which Kipling has become 'a caricature of his former self':

> KIPLING, RUDYARD, Poet Laureate and Recruiting Sergeant, was born all over the world, some eighteen years ago. After a lurid infancy at Westward Ho! in the company of Stalky & Co., he emigrated to India at the age of six and swallowed it whole. In the following year the British Empire was placed in his charge, and it is still there. A misgiving that England may have gone too far in the matter of self-esteem having struck him in 1897, he wrote 'The Recessional', but there are signs that he has since forgotten it.[9]

service. In a letter to Roberts, Kipling aligned himself as a fellow beleaguered patriot: 'If, as I believe, the effect of such pronouncements is to be judged by the amount of abuse elicited, it looks as if the reward of your long labours were in sight at last. I have never heard anything so taken to heart by *all* classes of society.'[14]

While Kipling sounded his warnings for the nation he could at least console himself with the thought that his own bit of the English landscape was safe. Bateman's remained a refuge from the turbulence of the world. To a neighbour in January 1913 he wrote 'from our tiny corner – *ille praetor omnes, Angulus ridet*' – an echo of lines from Horace, 'Ille terrarum mihi praeter omnes/angulus ridet', which translates as: 'That corner of the world smiles for me beyond all others.'[15]

The date of first publication of the *Just so Stories*, 1902, was also the date of a significant change in Kipling's personal and public identities. He was now attaching himself to Africa rather than India as the site of Britain's imperial ambitions, and the subtlety and sensitivity of *Kim* and many of his Indian poems and stories were replaced by an identity which at times comes close to Beerbohm's 1904 caricature of him (see p. 200).[16] As one of his editors has put it, his embitterment over the South African War 'embroiled Kipling in a mutually hostile relationship with the English liberal intelligentsia that to this day has never quite been resolved.'[17]

Kipling's personality was hardening. The pattern seems to be that he directed outwards, at opponents and enemies, the distress which he was unable to process within himself. The closing poem to 'How the Leopard got his Spots' is about a private moment between father and child. It could be an oblique additional testimony to his feeling for Josephine as well as about his surviving daughter, Elsie. The story was written down in 1899, the year of Josephine's death. The poem was written later, and has an English setting. The child in the poem is now identified with the 'Wise Baviaan'.

I AM the Most Wise Baviaan, saying in most wise tones,
  'Let us melt into the landscape – just us two by our lones.'

'Rudyard Kipling' by Max Beerbohm: 'Mr Rudyard Kipling takes a bloomin day aht, on the Blasted 'Eath, along with Britannia, 'is gurl' (1904)

Epilogue

People have come – in a carriage – calling. But Mummy is there . . .
Yes, I can go if you take me – Nurse says *she* don't care.
Let's go up to the pig-sties and sit on the farmyard rails!
Let's say things to the bunnies, and watch 'em skitter their tails!
Let's – oh, *anything*, daddy, so long as it's you and me,
And going truly exploring, and not being in till tea!
Here's your boots (I've brought 'em), and here's your cap and stick,
And here's your pipe and tobacco. Oh, come along out of it – quick!

The pigsties and farmyard rails are clearly part of a walk which father and child knew well on Kipling's own land around Bateman's. There are cancelled lines in the manuscript, Folio 31, which fill out the specific sense of place in the poem. The child is dressed for a muddy outing in the house's fields:

I've got on my dirtiest pinny, I've got on my weeding hat.
Let's go down to the ditches and scare up a water-rat.

And the child wants to see a 'baby teal on the mill dam' and an egg that one of the chickens has laid away from its run:

And there's a new laid astray, penny to me if I find it!
Bet you it's under the reaper, she's always clucking behind it.

Josephine had been dead for three years by the time Kipling purchased Bateman's. The child in the longer unpublished draft of the poem must have been Elsie, in the dirty pinny, at Bateman's, when she was about 5 years old. But the pressure of feeling within the final published poem argues against that. It allows the poem to stage an *imagined* 'what if?' situation. I think that in the revised poem Kipling briefly creates a happier alternative history in which Josephine has *not* died but is imagined still as a happy child in the landscape of Bateman's, sharing her father's fame and sunny good fortune.

In the later Kipling an obvious split has opened up between the creative writer and the political writer. He raged against the settlement of the South African War (which seemed to him a defeat for the English and a victory for the Dutch farmers) while retaining the ambivalent attachment to South Africa demonstrated by his behaviour over The Woolsack – of which Cecil Rhodes had left Kipling a life tenancy, and which Kipling continued to refer to as 'my house', though he chose not to return to it.[18] He was dismayed again by the triumph of the Liberal government which held office from 1906 to 1915. This government dashed all the hopes that Kipling had had for South Africa, deciding to return self-government to the former Boer Republics. To Edmonia Hill Kipling lamented that the work of years was 'chucked away for a whim of the English electorate'.[19] In his view this was a government which betrayed the British and their interests in South Africa. This was also a government which challenged the position of men of his class by eroding their property rights, restricting the role of the House of Lords as a bastion of resistance to the democratic left and allowing soft and lily-livered policies to prevail; Kipling had been anxiously husbanding and safeguarding his investments and was buying land round Bateman's as further security. He saw the whole country as weakened by this government: Bonar Law, Balfour and Lloyd George as Chancellor of the Exchequer contributed, in Kipling's view, to Britain's failure to build a standing army capable of confronting the perceived threat of German aggression. Kipling was enraged when Lloyd George introduced his 'People's Budget', whereby the Liberals' innovations – social reform, old age pensions and national insurance – were to be paid for by stringent taxation of the rich. At the same time the country was being put at risk by the same government's failure to reinforce the armed services by introducing national service.

He was further disheartened, from 1910 onwards, by what he saw as the treachery of the Irish in relation to the United Kingdom, and by the failure of the United States to recognise the threat of Germany. As many British Conservatives did, Kipling actively welcomed the outbreak

Epilogue

of war in 1914 as a crisis which forced a clear division between the patriotic and the treacherous. That confidence was broken, and the rest of his life irretrievably darkened, by the wasteful and avoidable death of John Kipling in 1915. There is no reference to the deaths of Josephine and John in *Something of Myself*. Emotional self-protection went with a sense of shapeliness and seemliness. The 'Something' in *Something of Myself* is primarily the life of a writer. Even the horrible bullying by Mrs Holloway is represented here as good training for a writer. The life of the family man takes second place.

Had he not had a famous and influential father, John Kipling would certainly not have secured his commission with the Irish Guards and been sent to the front; his weak eyesight would have excluded him from active service. Kipling's two-volume history of his son's regiment's engagement in the 1914–18 war, *The Irish Guards in the Great War*, published in 1923, was a labour of love and atonement. It draws on written and oral testimony from the soldiers themselves. Volume 2 of this history deals with the Second Battalion of the Irish Guards, the new battalion which John Kipling joined on 12 August 1915, in France. Kipling gave a tight-lipped account of his son's role in the Battle of Loos, 27 September 1915. It appears from his account that the Irish Guards were not in fact part of the plan of attack; the Scots Guards were ordered to attack the German line, and 'their rush took with them "some few Irish Guardsmen", with 2nd Lieutenants W.J.F. Clifford and J. Kipling of no. 2 Company who went forward not less willingly because Captain Cuthbert commanding the Scots Guards party had been Adjutant to the Reserve Battalion at Warley ere the 2nd Battalion was formed, and they all knew him'. Their advance brought them fatally 'well under machine-gun fire' and their consequent casualties included '2nd Lieutenant Kipling' who was 'wounded and missing'. The soldiers were totally unprepared for what they encountered. Kipling quotes one of them: 'Jerry did himself well at Loos upon us innocents. We went into it knowing no more than our own dead what was coming, and Jerry fair lifted us out of it with machine-guns. That was all there was to it *that* day.'[20] Kipling does not linger over his own son's death – it is finished and done with in the first twenty pages of this volume of the history – but he does point to the lies that had been told by the British command. The battle was paraded to the British public as a 'far-reaching success', while the reality was that both sides were picking up the pieces and the British back home rushed to improve their armaments. 'Meantime, men died.'[21]

On Kipling's death on 18 January 1936 it was recognised that literature had lost a major figure, but one who remained difficult to 'place'. As Edward Said has put it, 'he was accorded the honour reserved by Britain for its greatest writers: he was buried in Westminster Abbey. He has remained an institution in English letters, albeit one always slightly apart from the great central strand, acknowledged but slighted, appreciated but never fully canonized.'[22] Kipling was seldom other than protean and elusive. *Stalky & Co.* gave full expression to the Kipling who endorsed the British Empire's appetite for power, though it is important to recognise that the stories in this volume are not naively brutal and philistine.

The story 'Slaves of the Lamp I' makes use of Kipling's childhood spent partly with Morris and Burne-Jones, disciples of Ruskin. He knew Ruskin's work, and his study-mate George Beresford ('McTurk' in the stories) was a reader of Ruskin's *Fors Clavigera* (1871–8), while he himself, Kipling ('Beetle'), was a reader and disciple of Browning's poetry, especially the *Men and Women* (1855) volume. Ruskin's own faith in an alternative to capitalist society finds reflection in the sense of community which exists in Study Number 5. In an interview in 1900, a year after the publication of *Stalky & Co.*, Kipling's schoolfriend Lionel Dunsterville ('Stalky') stressed the remoteness of Study Number 5 from typical schoolboy life:

What must they [the other boys in the school] have thought of three youngsters who tried to model their lives – for a month or so at a time – on the maxims of Ruskin, varying the menu with a course of Carlyle – who decorated their study with a seagreen dado and Greek border – who spent their pocket money in buying prints of Medieval saints in the cult of Pre-Raphaelite art?[23]

'So far as the masters were concerned,' said Dunsterville, 'not one of them could ever get the better of Kipling'. Ruskin's violent criticism of the capitalist world is to some degree reflected in the enthusiasm with which the boys destroy the authority of some of the schoolmasters. 'Slaves of the Lamp I' is in part a revenge story, in which the three enlist an enraged Devonshire peasant in a plot to damage the cherished contents of the private study used by 'King', based on an English and Classics teacher at the school named William Crofts. A further twist is that it was Crofts who recognised the schoolboy Kipling's talent and encouraged him to read Browning, for which Kipling was eternally indebted. There is tension here between Kipling's love of belonging to an effective male group, Study Number 5, and his equally strong love of independence, like that of the Cat that Walked by Himself.

The political commitment of *Stalky & Co.* is made plain by the final story in the volume, 'Slaves of the Lamp II', where boys from the school, now adults, reminisce about Stalky's exploits and recount the tale of a successful military exercise in India which has recently been led by Stalky. Stalky had displayed 'Stalkiness' to the hilt, by setting two Indian regiments from two separate tribes in conflict with each other instead of with the British, much as Stalky as a schoolboy had set two adults – King the housemaster and a local Devonshire man called Rabbits Eggs – against each other instead of against the three inhabitants of Study Number 5. What looked like disobedience to authority at school has turned out to be perfect training for the military control of the empire.

The Kipling who admired 'Stalkiness' was in evidence when he wrote from Cape Town to H. G. Wells, on 28 January 1902, giving a prose version of the contempt for English dilatoriness in the face of international threat which he had recently expressed most vividly in his poem 'The Islanders', first published in *The Weekly Times* on 4 January 1902. Wells' *Anticipations* had aired the same anxiety, and Kipling was pleased to find that on this point their views coincided:

> Not all the truth in the world saves a man who interferes with the noble English pastime of watching games. *'Which has made us what we are!'* I am immensely pleased that you are in the game too. After the idiots have done rowing and swearing and prevaricating they'll begin to take stock of the situation.[24]

In absolute contrast with these themes, the *Just so Stories* bring into full view the Kipling who loved play, artistry, craftsmanship, ingenuity, and the free imaginative world which he could share with small children. This was the artist who explored the notions of talking animals, alternative versions of the creation myth, patterns, riddles and structural inventiveness, and celebrated and shared the pleasure he found in these things. The *Just so Stories* is a text from which the concerns of the empire are successfully excluded. The stories exist within the context of the collective anxiety experienced by the British in the late Victorian and Edwardian periods, but they are insulated from its impact. This strength is a key feature of Kipling's achievement in these jewel-like works of art.

ENDNOTES

The *Just so Stories* were first published as a collection of twelve stories (London: Macmillan, 1902). All quotations and references to the texts of the *Just so Stories* in this present book are from the World's Classics edition of Rudyard Kipling, *Just so Stories*, ed. with introduction and notes by Lisa Lewis (Oxford: Oxford University Press, 2009), cited in these notes as *JS*. This edition adds two later stories, 'The Tabu Tale' and 'Ham and the Porcupine', to the original twelve.

1 How the Whale got his Throat

1. *JS*, pp. 4–5.
2. *JS*, p. 5.
3. *JS*, p. 5
4. *JS*, pp. 6–7.
5. *Just so Stories*, British Library Add. MS 59840, folio 4 (hereafter cited as *Just so* MS).
6. *JS*, pp. 8–9.
7. *JS*, p. 10.
8. Rudyard Kipling, *Something of Myself* (London: Macmillan, 1937), p. 129 (hereafter cited as *Something of Myself*).
9. *JS*, p. 8 (and n. 221).
10. Angela Thirkell, *Three Houses* (London: Robin Clark, 1986), pp. 83, 88.
11. Quoted in Roger Lancelyn Green, *Kipling and the Children* (London: Elek, 1965), p. 171 (hereafter cited as Green, 1965).
12. Muhammad bin Khavendshah bin Mahmud, *The 'Rauzat-Us-Safa', or Garden of Purity* (London: Royal Asiatic Society, 1892) (hereafter cited as *Garden*). Part of 'The Butterfly that Stamped' comes from Part I, vol. ii, pp. 79–80. The Whale story may also owe something to the story of a whale swallowing whole ships in *The Surprising Adventures of Baron Munchausen* (1786).
13. Mrs Molesworth, *The Cuckoo Clock* (London: Macmillan, 1896). This book had been regularly reprinted since its first publication in 1877.
14. William Fordyce Mavor, *The English Spelling Book* (London: Longman, 1819), and *Mavor's First Book for Children, intended as an Introduction to a Correct Knowledge of the English Language* (Printed for the Booksellers, 1840).
15. Margaret Gatty, *Parables from Nature: With Notes on the Natural History* (London: George Bell, 1888). The Burne-Jones image is on p. 205.
16. *Something of Myself*, p. 21, and notes from Thomas Pinney, ed., *Something of Myself: and Other Autobiographical Writing by Rudyard Kipling* (Cambridge: Cambridge University Press, 1990), p. 15 and n. (hereafter cited as Pinney, ed., 1990).
17. Andrew Lycett, *Rudyard Kipling* (London: Weidenfeld & Nicolson, 1999), p. 81 (hereafter cited as Lycett, 1999).

18. *Something of Myself*, p. 15.
19. *Something of Myself*, p. 16.
20. Pinney, ed. (1990), p. 164.
21. Edward Said, *Culture and Imperialism* (London: Vintage, 1994), p. 161 (hereafter cited as Said, 1994).
22. Lord Birkenhead, *Rudyard Kipling* (London: Weidenfeld & Nicolson, 1978), p. 57 (hereafter cited as Birkenhead, 1978).
23. Birkenhead, 1978, p. 63.
24. For an excellent account of this see Charles Allen, *Kipling Sahib: India and the Making of Rudyard Kipling* (London: Little, Brown, 2007), pp. 164–74 (hereafter cited as Charles Allen, 2007).
25. Quoted from a letter to Edmonia Hill, 9 May 1888. *The Letters of Rudyard Kipling*, ed. by Thomas Pinney (London: Macmillan, 1990–2004), 1, p. 170 (hereafter cited as *Letters*, with volume and page number).
26. *Letters*, 2, p. 86.
27. Angus Wilson, *The Strange Ride of Rudyard Kipling* (London: Granada, 1977), p. 367 (hereafter cited as Wilson, 1977).
28. Philip Mason, *Kipling: The Glass, the Shadow and the Fire* (New York: Harper & Row, 1975), p. 94 (hereafter cited as Mason, 1975).
29. Mason, 1975, p. 94.
30. Lycett, 1999, p. 326.
31. Quoted in Charles Carrington, *Rudyard Kipling: His Life and Work* (Harmondsworth: Penguin, 1986), p. 241 (hereafter cited as Carrington, 1986). This biography was first published by Macmillan in 1955.
32. *Letters*, 2, p. 66.
33. Rudyard Kipling, *The Jungle Book* (London: Macmillan, 1947, hereafter cited as *Jungle Book 1*), and Rudyard Kipling, *The Second Jungle Book* (London: Macmillan, 1899, hereafter cited as *Jungle Book 2*).
34. From 'In Partibus', first published December 1889, in *The Cambridge Edition of the Poems of Rudyard Kipling*, ed. by Thomas Pinney (Cambridge: Cambridge University Press, 2013), 2, p. 1321 (hereafter cited as *Poems*, with volume and page number).
35. *Letters*, 2, p. 86.

2 How the Camel got his Hump

1. *JS*, pp. 13–14.
2. *Just so* MS, folio 16.
3. *JS*, p. 14.
4. *JS*, p. 15.
5. *JS*, p. 15.
6. *JS*, p. 18.
7. *JS*, p. 16.
8. *JS*, p. 20.
9. *Letters*, 2, p. 130.
10. John Lockwood Kipling, *Beast and Man in India* (London: Macmillan, 1891), p. 285 (hereafter cited as John Lockwood Kipling, 1891).
11. John Lockwood Kipling, 1891, p. 255.
12. Harry Ricketts, *The Unforgiving Minute: A Life of Rudyard Kipling* (London: Chatto & Windus, 1999, hereafter cited as Ricketts, 1999), pp. 202–3.
13. Ricketts, 1999, p. 203.
14. Charles Allen, 2007, p. 335.
15. *JS*, p. 22.
16. Rudyard Kipling, *The Cause of Humanity and Other Stories*, ed. by Thomas Pinney (Cambridge: Cambridge University Press, 2019), pp. 22–8, pp. 239–41.

17. Birkenhead, 1978, pp. 170, 177–8.
18. Rudyard Kipling, 'The House Surgeon', in *Actions and Reactions* (London: Macmillan, 1909), pp. 267–8.
19. Rudyard Kipling, *Life's Handicap* (London: Macmillan, 1908), p. 251 (hereafter cited as *Life's Handicap*).
20. *Life's Handicap*, p. 245.
21. *Something of Myself*, p. 3.
22. John Lockwood Kipling, 1891, p. 273.
23. See Martin Dubois, 'Anthropomorphism in *Alice's Adventures in Wonderland*', in *Discovering Literature: Romantics and Victorians* (British Library online), 15 May 2014.
24. Lewis Carroll, *Alice's Adventures in Wonderland and Through the Looking-Glass* (London: Macmillan, 1888), pp. 162–3 (hereafter cited as *Alice*, 1888).
25. Rudyard Kipling, *The Complete Stalky & Co.* (London: Macmillan, 1930), p. ix.

3 How the Rhinoceros got his Skin

1. *JS*, p. 23.
2. *Just so* MS, folio 22.
3. *JS*, p. 24.
4. *JS*, p. 26.
5. *JS*, p. 30.
6. *JS*, p. 27.
7. *JS*, p. 25.
8. *JS*, pp. 25, 30.
9. *JS*, p. 24.
10. *JS*, pp. 33–4.
11. J.M.S. Tompkins, *The Art of Rudyard Kipling* (London: Methuen, 1959), p. 56 (hereafter cited as Tompkins).
12. *Alice*, 1888, pp. 87, 91.
13. Birkenhead,1978, pp. 157–8.
14. Ricketts, 1999, p. 221.
15. Quoted in Birkenhead, 1978, p. 168.
16. Birkenhead, 1978, p. 167.
17. Birkenhead, 1978, p. 168.

4 How the Leopard got his Spots

1. *JS*, pp. 33–4.
2. Rudyard Kipling, *Wee Willie Winkie and Other Stories* (London: Macmillan, 1895), p. 284 (hereafter cited as *Wee Willie Winkie*).
3. *Wee Willie Winkie*, p. 284.
4. *JS*, p. 34.
5. *JS*, pp. 34–5.
6. See Miles Taylor, *Empress: Queen Victoria and India* (London: Yale University Press, 2019), pp. 128–9.
7. *JS*, p. 36.
8. Morton Cohen (ed.), *Rudyard Kipling to Rider Haggard: The Record of a Friendship* (London: Hutchinson, 1965).
9. *JS*, p. 38.
10. *JS*, pp. 41–2.
11. *JS*, pp. 35, 38.
12. *JS*, pp. 39–40.
13. *Jungle Book 2*, p. 19.
14. See *Something of Myself*, pp. 208–10.

15. *JS*, p. 41.
16. *JS*, pp. 41–2.
17. *JS*, pp. 42–3.
18. Lycett, 1999, p. 482.
19. *Letters*, 3, p. 38.
20. *Letters*, 3, p. 40n.
21. *Letters*, 1, pp. 97–8.
22. *Letters*, 1, p. 99.
23. *Letters*, 1, p. 100.

5 The Elephant's Child

1. *Just so* MS, folio 38.
2. *JS*, pp. 47–8.
3. *JS*, pp. 48–9.
4. *JS*, p. 50.
5. *JS*, p. 51. Kipling here may be recalling Lewis Carroll's 'The Pool of Tears', *Alice*, 1888, Chapter 2, where Alice tries to recite Isaac Watts' moralising hymn for children, 'How doth the little Busy Bee' but it emerges instead as 'How doth the little crocodile ...'. Carroll's parody stresses the crocodile's murderousness. '*How cheerfully he seems to grin,/ How neatly spreads his claws,/And welcomes little fishes in/With gently smiling jaws!*' (*Alice*, 1888, p. 18).
6. *JS*, pp. 52–3.
7. *JS*, p. 53.
8. *JS*, p. 54.
9. *JS*, pp. 53–8.
10. *JS*, p. 58.
11. *JS*, pp. 58–9.
12. *JS*, p. 56.
13. *JS*, p. 49.
14. *Something of Myself*, p. 149.
15. *Something of Myself*, pp. 173–4.
16. *Poems*, 1, pp. 614–15.
17. Ricketts, 1999, p. 236.
18. *Something of Myself*, p. 147.
19. *Poems*, 1, pp. 614–15.
20. Elliot L. Gilbert, *The Good Kipling* (Manchester: Manchester University Press), 1972, p. 19 (hereafter cited as Gilbert, 1972).
21. Carrington, 1986, p. 363.
22. John Lockwood Kipling, 1891, pp. 230–1.
23. John Lockwood Kipling, 1891, pp. 231–2.
24. John Lockwood Kipling, 1891, pp. 231–62.
25. Robert Buchanan, 'The Voice of the Hooligan', *The Contemporary Review* (December 1899).
26. Ricketts, 1999, p. 206.
27. Ricketts, 1999, p. 207.
28. Ricketts, 1999, p. 207.
29. Ricketts, 1999, p. 208.
30. Rudyard Kipling, *Many Inventions* (London: Macmillan, 1899), p. 205 (hereafter cited as *Many Inventions*).
31. *Many Inventions*, p. 202.
32. John Lockwood Kipling, 1891, pp. 313–14.
33. *Jungle Book 1*, p. 4.
34. *Jungle Book 1*, p. 5.

35. *Jungle Book 2*, p. 70.
36. *Jungle Book 2*, p. 221.
37. *Letters*, 2, p. 62.
38. *Letters*, 2, p. 62.
39. Said, 1994, p. 167.
40. *Letters*, 3, p. 11.
41. *Something of Myself*, p. 141.
42. Rudyard Kipling, *Kim* (London: Macmillan, 1901), pp. 120–2 (hereafter cited as *Kim*).
43. *Kim*, p. 413.
44. Wilson, 1977, p. 99.
45. *JS*, p. 62.

6 The Sing-Song of Old Man Kangaroo

1. *JS*, p. 63.
2. *JS*, p. 66.
3. *JS*, p. 64.
4. *Just so* MS, folio 48.
5. *JS*, pp. 65, 68.
6. *JS*, p. 68.
7. *JS*, p. 69.
8. Carrington, 1986, p. 367.
9. Quoted in Lycett, 1999, pp. 440–1.
10. *JS*, pp. 69, 72.
11. *JS*, p. 70.
12. *JS*, pp. 70, 71.
13. Gilbert, 1972, p. 77.
14. Gilbert, 1972, pp. 94–111.
15. Tompkins, p. 90.
16. Rudyard Kipling, *Traffics and Discoveries* (London: Macmillan, 1904), pp. 339–65 (hereafter cited as *Traffics and Discoveries*).
17. Ricketts, 1999, p. 9.
18. Letters to Rudolph Block, 16 May 1896, and Frederick Holbrook, 18 May 1896, in *Letters*, 2, pp. 240, 241.
19. *JS*, p. 73.
20. Elliot L. Gilbert, ed., *O Beloved Kids: Rudyard Kipling's Letters to his Children* (London: Little Books) 2009, p. 66 (hereafter cited as *O Beloved Kids*).
21. *O Beloved Kids*, pp. 66–7.
22. *O Beloved Kids*, pp. 57–8.
23. *O Beloved Kids*, pp.109–10.
24. *Letters*, 4, p. 107.

7 The Beginning of the Armadilloes

1. *JS*, pp. 75–6.
2. *JS*, p. 77.
3. *Letters*, 2, p. 217.
4. This view of it is proposed in an essay by Rosalind Meyer, 'But is it Art? An Appreciation of the *Just so Stories*', in *Kipling Journal*, December 1984.
5. *JS*, pp. 82–3.
6. *JS*, p. 87.
7. *JS*, p. 87.
8. *JS*, pp. 77–8.
9. *JS*, pp. 78, 79.

10. *JS*, p. 230.
11. *JS*, p. 88.
12. Rudyard Kipling, *The Day's Work* (London: Macmillan, 1904), p. 4 (hereafter cited as *The Day's Work*).
13. *The Day's Work*, pp. 42–3.
14. *The Day's Work*, p. 38.
15. *The Day's Work*, p. 40. See also the discussion of this in Tompkins, p. 192.
16. Gilbert, 1972, p. 129.
17. *JS*, p. 90.
18. Wilson, 1977, pp. 306–7.
19. Quoted from *The Poems of Richard Corbett*, ed. by J.A.W. Bennett and H.R. Trevor-Roper (Oxford: Clarendon Press, 1955), pp. 49–51.

8 How the First Letter was Written

1. *JS*, p. 91.
2. Quoted in *JS*, p. 231.
3. *JS*, p. 92.
4. *JS*, p. 93.
5. *JS*, pp. 96–7.
6. *JS*, p. 97.
7. *JS*, p. 95.
8. *JS*, p. 98.
9. *JS*, pp. 98–100.
10. *JS*, pp. 102–3.
11. *Something of Myself*, p. 13.
12. *JS*, p. 81.
13. *JS*, p. 103.
14. *JS*, pp. 104–5.
15. Lycett, 1999, p. 456.
16. *Traffics and Discoveries*, p. 233.
17. *Many Inventions*, p. 100.
18. *Many Inventions*, p. 107.
19. *Many Inventions*, p. 116.
20. *Something of Myself*, p. 210.
21. 'Proofs of Holy Writ', in *Kipling's Lost World*, ed. Harry Ricketts (Padstow: Tabb House, 1989), pp. 125–38.
22. *Something of Myself*, p. 206.
23. *Something of Myself*, pp. 207–8.
24. *Something of Myself*, p. 206.

9 How the Alphabet was Made

1. *JS*, pp. 109–10.
2. *JS*, p. 111.
3. *JS*, p. 114.
4. *JS*, pp. 125–7.
5. Carrington, 1986, p. 318n.
6. Carrington, 1986, pp. 318–20.
7. *Letters*, 2, p. 339.
8. Carrington, 1986, pp. 344–5.
9. Carrington, 1986, pp. 345–6.
10. Carrington, 1986, p. 350.
11. *JS*, pp. 107, 128.
12. *Traffics and Discoveries*, pp. 303, 305.

13. T.S. Eliot, *The Complete Poems and Plays* (London: Faber, 1969), pp. 171–2.
14. *Traffics and Discoveries*, p. 333.

10 The Crab that Played with the Sea

1. *JS*, pp. 129–30.
2. *JS*, p. 130.
3. *JS*, p. 132.
4. *JS*, p. 130.
5. Tompkins, p. 194.
6. *JS*, p. 130.
7. Tompkins, p. 195.
8. *JS*, p. 132.
9. *Letters*, 2, p. 77.
10. Tompkins, p. 195.
11. *JS*, p. 130.
12. Quoted in Green, 1965, p. 179.
13. W.W. Skeat, *Malay Magic* (London: Macmillan, 1900), pp. 3–4 (hereafter cited as Skeat, 1900).
14. *JS*, p. 134.
15. Skeat, 1900, p. 7.
16. *JS*, p. 139.
17. *JS*, p. 141.
18. *JS*, p. 139.
19. *JS*, pp. 143–4.
20. *JS*, p. 140.
21. *Letters*, 1, pp. 378–9.
22. Written in the Hotel du Grand Monarque, Chartres, 14 March 1925. *Letters*, 5, p. 212.

11 The Cat that Walked by Himself

1. *JS*, pp. 149–50.
2. Carrington, 1986, p. 432.
3. Carrington, 1986, p. 433.
4. Carrington, 1986, p. 437.
5. Lycett, 1999, p. 464.
6. Lycett, 1999, p. 464.
7. Quoted by Lycett, 1999, p. 464
8. *JS*, p. 150.
9. *JS*, p. 150.
10. See Jan Montefiore, '"Singing Magic": Women and Song in Kipling's Fiction', *Kipling Journal*, 93 (March, 2019), pp. 24–39.
11. *JS,* pp. 150–1.
12. Carrington, 1986, p. 587.
13. *JS*, p. 156.
14. Birkenhead, 1978, p. 169.
15. *JS*, p. 235 (quoted from the endnote by Lisa Lewis).
16. *JS*, p. 152.
17. Carrington, 1986, pp. 592–3.
18. Ricketts, 1999, p. 217.
19. *Something of Myself*, p. 184.
20. *JS*, p. 159.
21. *JS*, p. 155.
22. *Kim*, p. 203.
23. *Kim*, p. 204.
24. *Kim*, pp. 204–5.

25. *JS*, p. 154.
26. Quoted in Lycett, 1999, p. 324.
27. *Letters*, 4, pp. 79–80.
28. *O Beloved Kids*, p. 177.
29. Quoted in Lycett, 1999, pp. 615–16.
30. Hugh Brogan, 'The Great War and Rudyard Kipling', in Jan Montefiore, ed., *In Time's Eye: Essays on Rudyard Kipling* (Manchester: Manchester University Press, 2013), p. 76 (hereafter cited as Montefiore, 2013).
31. Montefiore, 2013, p. 77.
32. Montefiore, 2013, p. 78.
33. Quoted by Adam Nicolson in *The Hated Wife: Carrie Kipling, 1862–1939* (London: Short Books, 2001), p. 71.
34. *O Beloved Kids*, p. 218.
35. Lycett, 1999, p. 620.
36. Quoted in Lycett, 1999, p. 621.
37. *Letters*, 4, p. 339.
38. *Letters*, 4, p. 338.
39. *Letters*, 4, p. 402.
40. Lycett, 1999, p. 617.
41. *Letters*, 4, p. 340n.
42. *Poems*, 2, p. 1098.
43. Quoted in Lycett, 1999, p. 659.

12 The Butterfly that Stamped

1. *JS*, p. 169.
2. *JS*, p. 170.
3. Detailed endnote by Lisa Lewis, *JS*, pp. 235–6.
4. *JS*, p. 171.
5. Robert Browning, 'Solomon and Balkis', *The Poems*, ed. by John Pettigrew and Thomas Collins, vol. 2 (Harmondsworth, Penguin, 1981), pp. 668–70.
6. *JS*, p. 179.
7. *JS*, p. 174.
8. *JS*, p. 180.
9. *JS*, p. 182.
10. *Garden*, I, 2, pp. 79–80.
11. *Garden*, I, 2, p. 80.
12. *JS*, pp. 170–1.
13. *JS*, p. 172.
14. *JS*, p. 172.
15. *Something of Myself*, p. 52; Lycett, 1999, p. 175.
16. Rudyard Kipling, *Debits and Credits* (London: Macmillan, 1926), pp. 57–80 (hereafter cited as *Debits and Credits*).
17. *Something of Myself*, pp. 52–3.
18. Lycett, 1999, p. 176.
19. *Debits and Credits*, p. 61.
20. *Debits and Credits*, p. 65.
21. *Debits and Credits*, p. 240.
22. *Debits and Credits*, p. 248.
23. *Debits and Credits*, p. 250.
24. *Debits and Credits*, p. 173.
25. Quoted by Lycett, 1999, p. 717.
26. *Debits and Credits*, p. 399.
27. *Debits and Credits*, p. 413.

28. *Debits and Credits*, pp. 413–14.
29. George Orwell, 'Rudyard Kipling', in Andrew Rutherford, ed., *Kipling's Mind and Art* (Stanford, CA: Stanford University Press, 1966), pp. 70–1.
30. Lycett, 1999, p. 396.
31. Humphrey Carpenter, *Secret Gardens: The Golden Age of Children's Literature* (London: Allen & Unwin, 1985), p. 15.
32. Edward Said, *Orientalism* (Harmondsworth: Penguin Books, 1985), p. 227.
33. Lycett writes that '1908 was a crucial year as he adjusted from his bi-continental straddling of the world'. Lycett, 1999, p. 528.
34. Richard Gill, *Happy Rural Seat: The English Country House and the Literary Imagination* (New Haven, CT: Yale University Press, 1972), pp. 23–4.
35. Lycett, 1999, pp. 559–62.

13 The Tabu Tale and Ham and the Porcupine

1. *JS*, p. 189.
2. *JS*, pp. 189–90.
3. *JS*, p. 190.
4. *JS*, p. 192.
5. *JS*, p. 196.
6. *JS*, pp. 198–9.
7. *JS*, p. 208.
8. *JS*, pp. 193–4.
9. R.R.S. Baden-Powell, *Scouting for Boys* (first published 1908), ed. with an introduction by Elleke Boehmer (Oxford: Oxford University Press, 2004), pp. 6–7 (hereafter cited as *Scouting for Boys*). See also the discussion of Kipling's contribution to Baden-Powell's project in Hugh Brogan's illuminating study, *Mowgli's Sons* (London: Jonathan Cape, 1987).
10. *Scouting for Boys*, pp. 14–18.
11. Rudyard Kipling, *Rewards and Fairies* (London: Macmillan, 1910), p. 319.
12. *JS*, p. 213.
13. *JS*, pp. 213–14.
14. *JS*, pp. 216–17.
15. *JS*, p. 217.
16. *JS*, pp. 217–18.
17. *Letters*, 5, p. 218.

Epilogue

1. Tamara Gray, ed., *Just When Stories* (London: Beautiful Books, 2010), pp. 88–90.
2. A.A. Milne, *Winnie the Pooh* (London: Methuen, 1926); *The House at Pooh Corner* (London: Methuen, 1928); David Benedictus, *Return to Hundred Acre Wood* (London: Dutton, 2009).
3. *Letters*, 3, p. 37.
4. Quoted in Carrington, 1986, p. 595.
5. John Batchelor, *The Edwardian Novelists* (London: Duckworth, 1982), p. 137.
6. Writings in this genre were admirably discussed by Richard Gill in his pioneering work on this topic, *Happy Rural Seat* (New Haven, CT: Yale University Press, 1972).
7. G.H. Powell, introduction to George Chesney, *The Battle of Dorking* (London: Grant Richards, 1914), p. ix.
8. *Poems*, 1, pp. 559–62.
9. Quoted by Ricketts, 1999, p. 268.
10. M.P. Shiel, *The Yellow Danger* (London: Grant Richards, 1898), p. 338 (hereafter cited as Shiel, 1898).
11. Shiel, 1898, p. 347.

12. Rudyard Kipling, *From Sea to Sea, and Other Sketches*, Vol. I (London: Macmillan, 1901), p. 275 (hereafter cited as *From Sea to Sea I*).
13. *From Sea to Sea I*, p. 277.
14. *Letters*, 4, pp. 132–3 and note.
15. *Letters*, 4, p. 143 and note.
16. Max Beerbohm, *The Poets' Corner* (first published 1904, London: King Penguin, 1943), p. 24.
17. W.W. Robson, introduction to the World's Classics edition of *The Jungle Books* (Oxford: Oxford University Press, 2008), p. xii.
18. Thomas Pinney, introduction to Part Two of *Letters*, 3, p. 121.
19. *Letters*, 3, p. 215.
20. Rudyard Kipling, *The Irish Guards in the Great War*, vol. 2, *The Second Battalion* (London: Macmillan, 1923), pp. 11–12 (hereafter cited as *The Irish Guards*).
21. *The Irish Guards*, 2, p. 15.
22. Said, 1994.
23. Green, 1965, p. 65.
24. *Letters*, 3, p. 85.

SELECT BIBLIOGRAPHY

Baden-Powell, R.R.S., *Scouting for Boys* (first published 1908), ed. with an introduction by Elleke Boehmer. Oxford: Oxford University Press, 2004. Boehmer's commentary is helpful and illuminating.

Batchelor, John, *The Edwardian Novelists*. London: Duckworth, 1982. Includes a discussion of Kipling in an Edwardian context.

Batchelor, John, 'Kipling the Poet in Full', *Modern Language Review*, July 2014, pp. 663–73.

Batchelor, John, 'Dickens, Tennyson, Kipling', in Richard Bradford, ed., *A Companion to Literary Biography*. London: Blackwell/Wiley, 2019, pp. 489–509.

Birkenhead, Lord, *Rudyard Kipling*. London: Weidenfeld & Nicolson, 1978. The founding biography of Kipling, planned for publication in the 1940s. It was unaccountably blocked by Kipling's daughter, Mrs Elsie Bambridge, and was finally published some thirty years after completion, when both Birkenhead and Mrs Bambridge had died.

Booth, Howard J., ed., *The Cambridge Companion to Rudyard Kipling*. Cambridge: Cambridge University Press, 2011. Includes helpful essays by David Bradshaw, Jan Montefiore, Harry Ricketts and Bart Moore-Gilbert.

Brogan, Hugh, *Mowgli's Sons*. London: Jonathan Cape, 1987. Illuminating account of Baden-Powell's borrowings from Kipling's writings for training purposes in his Boy Scout movement.

Brogan, Hugh, 'The Great War and Rudyard Kipling', in Jan Montefiore, ed., *In Time's Eye: Essays on Rudyard Kipling*. Manchester: Manchester University Press, 2013, pp. 73–90. Brogan's important essay clarifies Kipling's response to the Great War of 1914–18 (in which his only son died). It is designed to 'rescue Kipling's reputation from ignorant libel'.

Bryant, Julius, and Weber, Susan, eds, *John Lockwood Kipling: Arts and Crafts in the Punjab and London*. New Haven, CT and London: Yale University Press, 1917. Informative and generously illustrated exhibition catalogue.

Bubb, Alexander, *Meeting without Knowing It: Kipling and Yeats at the Fin de Siècle*. Oxford: Oxford University Press, 2016. An ingenious double biography.

Carpenter, Humphrey, *Secret Gardens: The Golden Age of Children's Literature*. London: Allen & Unwin, 1985. Includes a helpful discussion of Kipling's writing for children.

Carrington, Charles, *Rudyard Kipling: His Life and Work*. Harmondsworth: Penguin, 1986 (first published in 1955). The authorised biography commissioned by Mrs Elsie Bambridge, Kipling's daughter, after she had suppressed the earlier biography by Lord Birkenhead.

Cohen, Morton, ed., *Rudyard Kipling to Rider Haggard: The Record of a Friendship*. London: Hutchinson, 1965.

Fleming, Mrs A.M. [Kipling's sister 'Trix'] 'Some Childhood Memories of Rudyard Kipling', *The Kipling Journal*, December 2019, pp. 25–40.

Gilbert, Elliot L., *The Good Kipling*. Manchester: Manchester University Press, 1972. Subtle essays on Kipling's more complex stories.

Select Bibliography

Gilbert, Elliot L., ed., *O Beloved Kids: Rudyard Kipling's Letters to his Children*. London: Little Books, 2009. Kipling's letters to Elsie and John Kipling.

Gill, Richard, *Happy Rural Seat: The English Country House and the Literary Imagination*. New Haven, CT: Yale University Press, 1972. Valuable account of the English country house in the literary imagination.

Green, Roger Lancelyn, *Kipling and the Children*. London: Elek, 1965. Discusses most of Kipling's writing for children.

Gross, John, ed., *Rudyard Kipling: The Man, His Work and His World*. London: Weidenfeld & Nicolson, 1972. Includes scholarly essays by Gillian Avery, Nirad Chaudhuri, Leon Edel, Philip Mason, Bernard Bergonzi and J.I.M. Stewart.

Karlin, Daniel, ed., *Rudyard Kipling*. Oxford: Oxford University Press, 1999. Judicious selection from Kipling's prose and verse, with helpful notes.

Keating, Peter, *Kipling the Poet*. London: Secker & Warburg, 1994. Sensitive biography which takes Kipling's poetry as the point of entry into his life.

Kemp, Sandra, *Kipling's Hidden Narratives*. Oxford: Basil Blackwell, 1988. Explores the psychic, religious and uncanny in Kipling's writing.

The Kipling Journal (published by the Kipling Society in four numbers annually, 1927 to present). Helpful contributions from a wide range of Kipling readers, both academic and 'lay'. See especially the volume entitled 'Rudyard Kipling and the Great War', *The Kipling Journal*, 89 (361). This whole issue gives contextual information on Kipling's response to the 1914–18 war and adds biographical information about John Kipling.

Knoepflmacher, U.C., 'Kipling's "Just-So" Partner: The Dead Child as Collaborator and Muse', *The Kipling Journal*, December 2016, pp. 25–48. (This essay first appeared in the periodical *Children's Literature* in 1997.) Josephine ('Effie') Kipling is imagined as a collaborator with the Just so Stories.

Lycett, Andrew, *Rudyard Kipling*. London: Weidenfeld & Nicolson, 1999. Substantial and thoroughly researched chronicle of Kipling's life.

Mallett, Phillip, *Rudyard Kipling: A Literary Life*. London: Palgrave Macmillan, 2003. Helpful biographical study which reads his work in the context of his life within a concise chronological narrative.

Mason, Philip, *Kipling: The Glass, the Shadow and the Fire*. New York: Harper & Row, 1975. Helpful biography by a writer with deep experience of India.

Montefiore, Jan, *Rudyard Kipling*. Tavistock: Northcote House, 2007. Concise and perceptive critical study of Kipling.

Montefiore, Jan, ed., *In Time's Eye: Essays on Rudyard Kipling*. Manchester: Manchester University Press, 2013. Valuable collection of essays by major Kipling scholars.

Moore-Gilbert, B.J., *Kipling and 'Orientalism'*. London: Croom Helm, 1986.

Nicolson, Adam, *The Hated Wife: Carrie Kipling, 1862–1939*. London: Short Books, 1901. Challenges the dislike with which Carrie Kipling is regarded by many writers on Kipling.

Pinney, Thomas, ed., *Something of Myself and Other Autobiographical Writings by Rudyard Kipling*. Cambridge: Cambridge University Press, 1990. Helpfully annotated edition of Kipling's autobiographical writings.

Pinney, Thomas, ed., *The Letters of Rudyard Kipling*, in six volumes. London: Macmillan, 1990–2004.

Pinney, Thomas, ed., *The Cambridge Edition of the Poems of Rudyard Kipling*, in three volumes. Cambridge: Cambridge University Press, 2013.

Pinney, Thomas, ed., *Rudyard Kipling: The Cause of Humanity and Other Stories: Uncollected Prose Fictions*. Cambridge: Cambridge University Press, 2019. Collection of fugitive or unpublished Kipling pieces, including two tales which reflect Kipling's depressive episodes in his early life: 'De Profundis (A Study in a Sick Room)' and 'Till the Day Break'.

Raine, Craig, ed., *A Choice of Kipling's Prose*. London: Faber, 1987.

Raine, Craig, ed., *Rudyard Kipling: Selected Poetry*. Harmondsworth: Penguin, 1992. This edition is prefaced by an excellent essay on Kipling's standing as a poet.

Select Bibliography

Ricketts, Harry, *The Unforgiving Minute: A Life of Rudyard Kipling*. London: Chatto & Windus, 1999. Gracefully written and well-planned biography.

Rutherford, Andrew, ed., *Kipling's Mind and Art*. Stanford, CA: Stanford University Press, 1964. Includes contributions from Edmund Wilson, George Orwell and Mark Kinkead-Weekes.

Said, Edward, *Orientalism*. Harmondsworth: Penguin, 1985 [first published 1978]. This study proposed that in Kipling's work the Eastern 'other' is displayed as incapable of writing about itself.

Said, Edward, *Culture and Imperialism*. London: Chatto & Windus, 1993. Kipling may be 'a Tory imperialist' who 'assumes a basically uncontested empire', but Kim remains a great work of art.

Shires, Linda, ed., *Victorians Reading the Romantics: Essays by U.C. Knoepflmacher*. Columbus, OH: Ohio State University Press, 2016. Includes Knoepflmacher's essay on 'Kipling as Browning: From Parody to Translation'.

Sullivan, Zoreh T., *Narratives of Empire: The Fictions of Rudyard Kipling*. Cambridge: Cambridge University Press, 1993. This study explores 'the contradictions of imperial fantasy' in Kipling's writing. For this critic, *Kim*, in particular, is 'both a fantasy of regression and a fantasy of realized ideology'.

Taylor, Miles, *Empress: Queen Victoria and India*. New Haven, CT and London: Yale University Press, 2019.

Tompkins, J.M.S., *The Art of Rudyard Kipling*. London: Methuen, 1959. 'Art' is the key word in Miss Tompkins' title. This famous study, subtle, elegant, and consistently objective, remains an indispensable reading of Kipling's work.

Walsh, Sue, *Kipling's Children's Literature: Language, Identity, and Constructions of Childhood*. Farnham: Ashgate, 2010. Well-informed and careful account of Kipling's writing for children.

Wilson, Angus, *The Strange Ride of Rudyard Kipling*. London: Secker & Warburg, 1977. Angus Wilson's early childhood (in Africa) had parallels with Kipling's childhood in India, and that is reflected in this personal and sympathetic biography.

INDEX

Index

Index

Index

Index